D0065121

MULTIPLE SCLEROSIS

Other titles in Diseases and People

AIDS
0-7660-1182-8

ALLERGIES
0-7660-1048-1

ANOREXIA AND BULIMIA
0-7660-1047-3

ASTHMA
0-89490-712-3

CANCER
0-7660-1181-X

**CARPAL TUNNEL SYNDROME AND
OTHER REPETITIVE STRAIN INJURIES**
0-7660-1184-4

CHICKENPOX AND SHINGLES
0-89490-715-8

COMMON COLD AND FLU
0-89490-463-9

DEPRESSION
0-89490-713-1

DIABETES
0-89490-464-7

EPILEPSY
0-7660-1049-X

**FOOD POISONING AND
FOODBORNE DISEASES**
0-7660-1183-6

HEART DISEASE
0-7660-1051-1

HEPATITIS
0-89490-467-1

LYME DISEASE
0-7660-1052-X

**MEASLES AND
RUBELLA**
0-89490-714-X

MENINGITIS
0-7660-1187-9

MONONUCLEOSIS
0-89490-466-3

RABIES
0-89490-465-5

**SEXUALLY TRANSMITTED
DISEASES**
0-7660-1050-3

SICKLE CELL ANEMIA
0-89490-711-5

TUBERCULOSIS
0-89490-462-0

—Diseases and People—

MULTIPLE SCLEROSIS

Edward Susman

Enslow Publishers, Inc.

40 Industrial Road   PO Box 38
Box 398   Aldershot
Berkeley Heights, NJ 07922   Hants GU12 6BP
USA   UK

http://www.enslow.com

Library of Congress Cataloging-in-Publication Data

Susman, Edward.
     Multiple sclerosis / Edward Susman.
        p. cm.—(Diseases and people)
     Includes bibliographical references and index.
     Summary: Discusses the history, symptoms, diagnosis, treatment, and future research
of multiple sclerosis.
     ISBN 0-7660-1185-2
     1. Multiple sclerosis—Juvenile literature. [1. Multiple sclerosis. 2. Diseases.] I. Title.
II. Series.
RC377.S87   1999
616.8'34—dc21   99-17210
                                                    CIP

Printed in the United States of America

10 9 8 7 6 5 4 3

To Our Readers:
All Internet addresses in this book were active and appropriate when we went to press. Any
comments or suggestions can be sent by e-mail to Comments@enslow.com or to the address
on the back cover.

Illustration Credits: Courtesy of the National Multiple Sclerosis Society

Cover Illustration: Courtesy of the National Multiple Sclerosis Society
In the cover photo, a young woman with multiple sclerosis shops at a department store.

Contents

Acknowledgments

Multiple sclerosis is a devastating disease, and knowledge about the disease and its treatment is in constant flux. I thank the people who helped me gather the information, especially the staff at the National Multiple Sclerosis Society who spent hours checking facts and encouraging my work. I want to thank my wife, Carolyn, and my children, Perrie and Ric, for their assistance in keeping stacks of notes and magazines safe, making numerous trips to libraries, and protecting my notes from the antics of Sam, our Siamese cat.

I am indebted to all the people who offered wise help and assistance for this book. If any errors were made, it is the fault of the gatherer, not the wonderful people who gave the information to me.

MULTIPLE SCLEROSIS

What is it? A chronic, often disabling condition of the central nervous system (brain, spinal cord, and optic nerves). In multiple sclerosis, brain impulses fail to reach arms, legs, or eyes.

Who gets it? More women than men, usually striking between the ages of twenty and forty, though individuals are diagnosed as young as nine or as old as seventy. At least three hundred fifty thousand people in the United States have multiple sclerosis.

How do you get it? No one knows for sure. However, symptoms result from multiple areas of patchy scarring (sclerosis) of the insulation (myelin) that surrounds nerve fibers. This is similar to loss of insulation material around a telephone cable, which interferes with transmission of messages. Most recent studies indicate that nerve fibers, as well as the nerve covering, are also destroyed. Some people have an inherited tendency to develop multiple sclerosis. However, no one knows exactly what inherited genes make a person susceptible to multiple sclerosis. For those who are susceptible to the disease, an infectious agent is required to trigger the multiple sclerosis response.

What are the symptoms? Weakness, which can progress to paralysis in arms or legs; loss of balance; difficulty in speaking; double vision; blurry vision; blindness; problems in controlling one's bladder; numbness and tingling. Symptoms may be mild, such as numbness in the limbs, or severe, such as paralysis or loss of vision. The progress, duration, or severity of these symptoms cannot be predicted.

How can it be treated? Various drugs such as steroids can treat the symptoms; newer therapies such as beta interferons and a polypeptide can reduce the number and severity of attacks. They may also slow the disease progression. Exercise and physical therapy can also help maintain strength.

How can it be prevented? No one knows.

1

What Is Happening to Me?

Roger Kennedy was confused and anxious. He awoke one morning twenty years ago and realized that there was something wrong with his vision. Everything was blurry, as if he were looking through eyeglasses with the wrong prescription. But after a few days, Kennedy's vision cleared. He returned to work at his manufacturing center in West Virginia.

Kennedy did not know it, and neither did the doctors he consulted, but the blurred vision was his first sign of multiple sclerosis (MS).

Meanwhile, Kennedy continued his work and went on hiking and hunting trips in the Appalachian hills near his home.

Again, without warning, another problem arose—this time a feeling of overwhelming fatigue. After a while the fatigue went away. Kennedy renewed his normal routine. He asked his doctors about these events, but they did not have any solid answers.

Years passed and then strange symptoms appeared. His hands and legs would suddenly feel numb, or he would have a sense of "pins and needles" in his arms and legs, hands and feet. Kennedy would wait for these symptoms to pass, and then he would try to get on with his life.

When he started having trouble walking, Kennedy knew he had to seek help again. "I was afraid to walk more than a quarter of a mile because I was unsure that I would make it home," he recalls today.[1]

With his condition worsening, Kennedy asked his doctor to check him into a hospital and find out what was wrong. He was given many diagnostic tests, but the results offered no conclusions. His doctors could not make a diagnosis. The symptoms that Kennedy was experiencing could have been caused by any number of problems, but when doctors tested Kennedy for those problems they came up empty.

Symptoms Come and Go

MS is a disease that is marked by symptoms that come and go. The symptoms can get quite severe and limit a person dramatically. People can go to sleep feeling fine and wake up unable to move their legs. Then the disease symptoms may slowly disappear.

At the time Kennedy went to his doctors, they were not sure what was going on. The vague symptoms changed without any apparent reason. The doctors were baffled. The doctors did not know they were dealing with MS, so they looked for other causes. The failure of his doctors to find out and explain what was wrong with him made Kennedy discouraged and concerned about his physical and mental health.

"I thought I was going crazy. I was having all these symptoms and still had no idea what was causing them," he said. In fact, a lot of patients—and sometimes their doctors—think undiagnosed multiple sclerosis patients may have mental disorders rather than an actual physical illness.

Often, the complaints are passed off by doctors who think the problem "is all in the head" of the patient. In a way, they are right. The problem is in the brain, but it is unrelated to mental activity.[2]

After ten days in a West Virginia hospital, Kennedy was exhausted by his illness. He was frustrated by lack of progress in finding out what was wrong with him. Worst of all, he was not getting any better. The West Virginia hospital and doctors decided that Kennedy should go to a hospital in Cleveland, Ohio, where experts in neurology—the study of the nervous system, including the brain—could try to figure out what was happening to him.

Neurologists there were finally able to put a name to Kennedy's illness—multiple sclerosis.

MS Today

Doctors have more questions about multiple sclerosis than they have answers.

MS is an unpredictable, chronic, and often disabling disease of the central nervous system. The central nervous system includes the brain, the spinal cord, and the optic nerves.

MS does not affect every person the same way. It is several different kinds of disease. There are mild forms of the disease that barely cause affected persons any difficulty for their entire lives. There are intermediate forms of the disease in which new medications can slow the slide to disability. And there is a progressive form of the disease that even the new medications available today cannot combat.

Until 1993 all doctors could do to treat MS was to provide drugs that targeted the symptoms as they occurred. There was nothing available to fight the disease process itself. After years of testing, doctors were finally able to report that they had found a substance that could actually affect the course of MS.

Today, three different drugs are being used by people such as Roger Kennedy to try and keep the illness quiet in the body. When MS symptoms subside, doctors call the condition remission—the obvious signs of the disease have gone away, but the disease is still present.

There is no cure for MS. The damage to the body that is caused by MS cannot yet be reversed. However, the quality of life for people with MS can be improved.

Since receiving medication, Kennedy has expanded his manufacturing business and opened a home-hardware center.

Multiple sclerosis affects different people in different ways. This woman, who has multiple sclerosis, explains disabilities to children, using a disabled doll.

He has resumed taking long hikes, confident he will be able to make it all the way home again.

"I feel I have more control over my life now," Kennedy said. "I'm no longer inhibited from doing the things that I enjoy."

For now, Kennedy is an MS success story.

MS is baffling and can be frustrating for those who have the disease. It is also frustrating to the medical detectives still on the case, trying to solve the mystery of MS.

2

MS: A New Disease or an Old One?

Before the nineteenth century, there are few references to the disease known as multiple sclerosis. The only early description of a person suffering a disease that could be MS occurs in the chronicle of the life of a Dutch woman, Lydwina of Scheiden, who lived in Holland in the 1400s.

Lydwina's life story was recorded by monks who described the holy woman's lifelong activities. The monks believed her tireless attempts to tend to those suffering from illness and hunger, despite her own physical ailments, made her worthy of sainthood. She was declared a saint and, because she was often depicted ice-skating, she is now considered the patron saint of ice-skaters.

One scene of Lydwina being carried off the ice testifies, some doctors believe, to falls that occurred because of MS attacks.

Between the time of Lydwina and the early nineteenth century, almost nothing is written about people with MS.

"Clearly," said Dr. Stephen Reingold, vice-president for research at the National Multiple Sclerosis Society in New York, "MS seems to have existed . . . probably at the time of Lydwina. It is likely that MS existed before Lydwina, although we have no written documentation of it." [1]

The First MS Diary

The first recorded MS diary—a chronicle of the symptoms of the disease—belonged to an Englishman, Sir Augustus D'Este, a relative of King George III. D'Este had just attended the funeral of a friend in December 1822 when he suffered a vision problem, called retrobulbar neuritis.[2]

Retrobulbar neuritis occurs when a part of the optic nerve becomes inflamed. The optic nerve connects the eye to the brain. When light energy is received in the eye, a series of events that occur at the cellular level changes light energy into chemical energy. The optic nerve sends the signals caused by this conversion to the brain. The brain translates the energy into vision.

When the optic nerve becomes inflamed, there is a rapid loss of vision and pain when moving the eyeball. In two to eight weeks, vision returns—often fairly completely without any treatment.[3]

Sir Augustus D'Este was twenty-eight years old when that first bout of MS struck. His eyesight recovered, but four years later he recorded further problems with his eyes. Over the years he described weakness, numbness, difficulty in walking, painful spasms, and depression. These symptoms frequently occur in people with MS.

In 1848, D'Este died when he was fifty-four, before the disease he suffered from had a formal name. However, the descriptions of his illness in the diary were so precise and so typical of MS, that later scientific investigators determined that he, indeed, had MS, and his diary is considered the world's first MS diary.

Today, there are many theories of how the disease, now known as MS, was spread around the world. One theory that has gained some credence involves the Vikings.

The Role of the Vikings

Vikings were pirates and warriors that lived in Scandinavia. They raided and plundered Europe from the late 700s to about 1100. This period in history is known as the Viking Age. Viking raids occurred frequently in the British Isles and in northern France. Viking adventurers sailed across the Atlantic and established colonies in Iceland and Greenland and even visited North America five hundred years before Columbus. The Vikings established colonies that were the origins of Russia, and these raiders even appeared in the Mediterranean and the Holy Land. They left their genetic mark on the lands that they entered.

The color of our eyes, the shape of our faces, and the hues of our skin are all determined by genes—our genetic makeup. We inherit genes from our mothers and fathers, and they carry genes from their parents and grandparents, and so on. Our genetic makeup is influenced by genes that were carried by our ancestors hundreds, even thousands, of years ago. Some researchers now think that the Vikings may have carried the genes that make a person vulnerable to multiple sclerosis.

The Vikings theory is one of many unproven theories that speculates on how the disease spread. Some people have suggested that environmental conditions such as climate or pollution caused the disease. Others suggest that sunshine, or lack of it, causes MS. Today, genetic theories are in the forefront.[4]

If the disease is a genetic influence of the Vikings, it might explain why MS occurs frequently in Scandinavia. The Vikings were fierce, warlike people who raided communities in Europe and the British Isles. The women there bore Vikings' children and produced a new generation of people with the genetic influence toward MS.

The descendants of the Vikings—particularly Englishmen and Scandinavians—settled in the New World of North America and Australia, and they took the MS genes along with them. Then, the theory contends, sometime before teenage years, some of these descendants became infected with a virus or bacterium. The combination of the infection and the genetic susceptibility (the tendency toward MS) began causing inflammation of nerve insulation in the central nervous system.

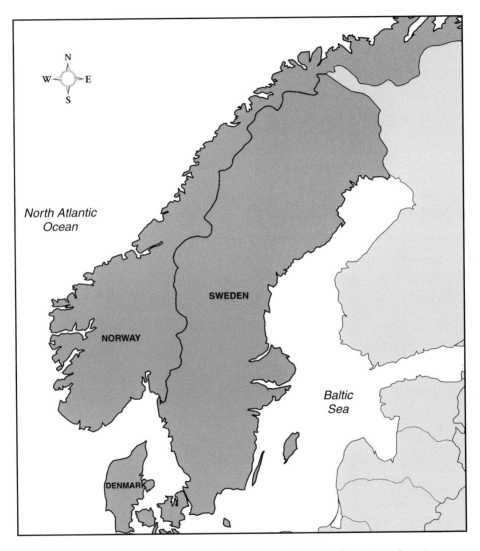

Some researchers believe that the Vikings, who were from Scandinavia (Denmark, Norway, and Sweden), carried the genes that make a person susceptible to multiple sclerosis.

The inflammation caused the symptoms of MS. So far, scientists know that there are at least nineteen different gene areas that may contribute to susceptibility to MS. However, no one knows what infectious agents might trigger the attacks of MS.[5]

A Disease Emerges

In the 1800s people with MS did not even have a name for their disease. While Sir Augustus D'Este was still recording information in his diary, other researchers were trying to determine what the disease was that they were beginning to see in some of their patients.

As D'Este diligently wrote his diary, doctors in England and in the rest of Europe were baffled by other patients with similar problems. The patients would have sudden vision problems. After a few weeks the vision troubles would end. They would suffer from unexplained weakness or numbness or tingling fingers and toes. These conditions, too, would slowly vanish. Some patients, however, would follow a generally downward course. Their arms and legs would become useless. They would become bedridden and would develop illnesses and die.

After the patients died, some of the doctors performed autopsies on them. These early autopsies helped researchers discover what was going on in the body that caused the symptoms of multiple sclerosis.

In London in 1837, Sir Robert Carswell, a professor of pathologic anatomy at University College, published the first anatomical description of MS. Carswell, a medical illustrator, drew pictures of the nerves of patients with these symptoms. He illustrated that these nerves were diseased, discolored, and withered.

At about the same time, Jean Cruveilhier, a professor of pathologic anatomy in Paris, published similar illustrations of the nerves of his patients. Cruveilhier also included a medical history of patients alongside his autopsy findings, giving a better picture of the disease.[6]

A complete picture of MS was not completed until one of the great doctors of the nineteenth century, Jean-Martin Charcot, began work at the famous Salpetriere Hospital in Paris.

Charcot was born in 1825, three years after D'Este began his diary, and rose to become one of the most respected men of medicine in the world. Today he is considered the father of modern neurology.

During the time he worked at Salpetriere Hospital, 1862 to 1870, Charcot studied the earlier work of Carswell and Cruveilhier. Charcot also had his own patients who were suffering from the baffling and changing disorder.

In 1868, about twenty years after the death of D'Este, Charcot published his studies. He described *sclerose en plaques*—"scarring in patches" —in the pathways of the body's central nervous system. When patients suffered multiple sclerose en plaques, Charcot said the patients then began having symptoms of the disease—multiple sclerosis.[7]

At the time Charcot identified MS as a disease, there were places in the world that had not previously seen the disease. One example was Australia. The first case of MS was not

MS Can Strike Anyone

The most susceptible people for multiple sclerosis are women of northern European-Scandinavian descent. However, the disease can strike anyone of most any age, race, or nationality.

Because the disease is so often considered a "white women's disease," diagnosis of MS in persons of color sometimes takes longer because the patient or the doctor will not think that MS is the cause.

In a study, Christine Loveland of Shippensburg University in Pennsylvania found that African Americans often took years to be diagnosed—including one woman who was not diagnosed as having multiple sclerosis until twenty-six years after her first attack of vision-threatening optic neuritis, a common MS symptom.

Loveland said one African-American woman with MS had problems convincing her mother that she had MS. The patient said her mother still believes the disease affects only white women and that her daughter caught the disease from living and working around white women.[8]

identified in Australia until 1886. It is possible other earlier cases went undetected.

However, the discovery of MS in Australia follows the genetic linkage to the Vikings. Aside from the native population of Australia, the main settlers of the continent came from the British Isles. The British Isles were one of the frequent places that the Vikings raided.

Changing Treatments and Theories

As theories for the causes of MS have varied over the years, so have the treatment approaches. In the 1890s, MS was attributed to overexertion. Therefore, patients thought to be suffering from MS were treated with herbs and bed rest. From the time of diagnosis, a person's life expectancy with MS was about five years.[9]

By the early 1900s doctors believed that the cause of MS was some unknown toxin, or poison, in the blood. They thought treatment with purgatives—drugs that made a person vomit or induced bowel evacuation—or stimulants were best able to handle symptoms of the disease. Life expectancy was extended to about ten years following diagnosis.

Each generation of doctors and researchers brought new ideas. In the 1920s and 1930s, specialists in treating the disease believed that MS was caused by some kind of infectious organism. They believed that a bacterium or a virus invaded the body and caused the symptoms seen in MS. Patients were treated with antisyphilis drugs. Syphilis, a bacteria-caused sexually transmitted disease, caused some symptoms that are similar to the symptoms of MS. Other MS patients were injected with typhoid vaccine in order to raise the body temperature in a treatment known as fever therapy. Patients were administered antibiotics and blood transfusions. Still, the result was the same: The disease progressed.

At the time of World War II, doctors became convinced that MS was caused by poor circulation and blood clots in the brain. In order to prevent these clots, blood thinners were prescribed for people with MS. That therapy did not work, either. However, better hospital care and treatment of the symptoms of the disease gave patients a better chance of living. Life expectancy after diagnosis rose to eighteen years.

For the next twenty years, from the 1950s through the 1970s, doctors treating MS patients believed that the disease was some form of allergic reaction. Doctors prescribed antihistamines, vitamins, and steroids to combat the conditions. The treatments did not cure the disease and did not stop its progression. Better hospitalization procedures and infection control helped extend the MS patient's life expectancy after diagnosis to about twenty-five years.

Today, most MS patients have essentially a normal life expectancy. MS is now looked at as an immune-system disorder. The immune system is designed to attack foreign substances that invade the body. When the immune system goes awry, certain immune-system substances attack healthy tissue such as myelin, the sheath surrounding nerve fibers. Drugs that directly attack the disease at a molecular level are slowing the progression of MS.

Most people who have multiple sclerosis have a normal life expectancy. Here, a past National Multiple Sclerosis Society "Father of the Year" begins his day while his son looks on.

Diaries Remain Important in Diagnosis

Even in the late twentieth century, some ways of detecting MS have not changed. Like Augustus D'Este's technique in 1822, one of the best ways of documenting MS is through a personal diary, such as one written by a college student, Dylan Humphrey.

On July 4, 1995, the anniversary of the birth of the United States, Dylan Humphrey found out that he was an unusual person. He was a young man, twenty-one years old, and he had multiple sclerosis.

In his public diary of his personal case of MS, Humphrey wrote: "I woke up the next afternoon. I blinked. Huh? I couldn't see out of my right eye. Hello optic neuritis, inflammation of the optic nerve."[10]

Humphrey, a student at Swarthmore College in Swarthmore, Pennsylvania, said, "I am quite the unique individual. MS usually strikes women. I'm a twenty-one-year-old man. I kinda see it as my punishment for wanting to be different than everyone else." Humphrey enjoys being an individualist—different from the rest of the students, even in illness.

Some people try to hide or disguise their illnesses. Others such as Humphrey believe that by being public about their disorder, they can help others cope with multiple sclerosis. They also can help people who do not have the disease understand what is happening to those who are ill.

Humphrey discussed his history of MS in diary form. He writes about his various flares of disease on the Internet, giving thousands of people the opportunity to follow the course of his disease with him.

3

What Is
Multiple Sclerosis?

In 1989, Joyce Goike of Clay, New York, a small community near Syracuse, was told she had multiple sclerosis. Aside from family and friends, she kept the news of her illness to herself, until 1997, when she finished her last year as a member of the Onondaga County Legislature.

Her disease had progressed to the point where she could no longer go to the regular meetings. Once an active gardener, Goike now requires a walker. Climbing stairs is nearly impossible. Her cane is useless unless someone also assists her. In the past two years, falls had resulted in broken ankles, wrists, and feet, and she also separated her shoulder when she fell while preparing supper.

"I can be standing still one moment and be flying across the room the next," said the fifty-seven-year-old woman who, nevertheless, still manages to operate a greenhouse business with her husband, Bill.

"I have never said, 'Why me?' I still have a lot of beauty in my life and I haven't let this thing take over. I talk to God more and more these days. I cry sometimes, but I think that's a good thing because I shouldn't hold it in. And I laugh, too, because you have to laugh."[1]

Joyce Goike's story is typical of people with MS in that the disease does not follow a predictable course. "There is no road map for MS," is the description other people with the disease have come to use. One never knows if she will be able to make the dinner date next week, dinner that night, or attend her daughter's wedding six months in the future.

A Central Nervous System Disorder

The central nervous system includes the brain, spinal cord, and optic nerves. Nerves carry messages between the brain and the rest of the body, including arms, legs, eyes, and mouth. Nerves are like telephone cables, sending messages to and from the brain at lightning speed to the hands and fingers, feet and toes.

The nerves are protected by a covering, similar to the way telephone wires are encased in a plastic covering. If that nerve covering, known as myelin, is disrupted or destroyed, some messages can get blocked, slowed, or rerouted. When this happens in a telephone system, you may not hear a word of a sentence or the sound may be fuzzy.

In MS, the protective insulation—myelin—around nerve

fibers breaks down, allowing nerve fibers to become inflamed. Myelin is destroyed and is replaced by scars of hardened patches of tissue. That process is called sclerosis.

When that happens to a nerve, impulses from the brain are disrupted. Instead of picking up a cup of coffee, a person's hand may suddenly jerk or spasm, knocking over the cup. It is also possible that nothing will happen, the hand just will not get the message from the brain. That becomes frustrating to the person with MS. Can you imagine wanting to change the television channel and seeing the television remote control on the arm of the chair next to you, but you cannot move your hand to pick up the device?

Most scientists now believe that MS symptoms are the result of numerous breaks in that protective covering on the nerves. That's how MS gets its name. Multiple—meaning many. Sclerosis—meaning scars. Many scars. Multiple sclerosis.

The patches can occur on any nerve system. When they occur on the optic nerve, vision is affected. When the patches occur on other nerves, messages from the brain to other areas of the body are cut off, distorted, or disrupted. Patients with MS suddenly find they are weak, or cannot walk, speak, or use their arms.

Newer research reported in 1997 contends that not only are there breaks in the myelin covering on nerves, but the nerves themselves are severed. These severed nerves can result in permanent loss of function for the patient. Instead of having

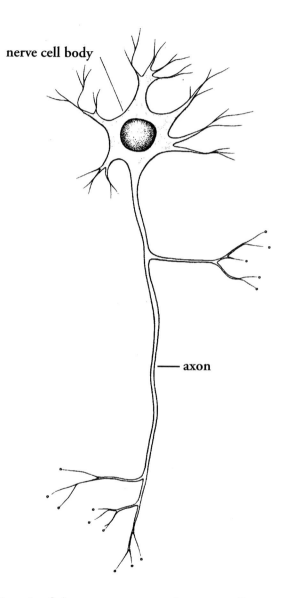

The basic unit of the nervous system, the nerve cell, carries messages throughout the body. Myelin covers the nerve's axon. When myelin is damaged, some messages can be disrupted.

difficulty walking, the patient cannot walk at all and needs a wheelchair. These newer reports are still being debated.[2]

The new theory may lead to better treatment. "If you don't know what is precisely wrong, you cannot design adequate therapies," said Dr. Richard Rudick, director of the Cleveland Clinic's Mellen Center, one of the largest programs in the country for research and the treatment of multiple sclerosis.

Bruce Trapp, chairman of the department of neurosciences at the Cleveland Clinic, said, "If you look at the nerve fibers and the myelin as wires and insulation, MS is usually viewed as a disease that destroys the insulation. Now we are saying MS cuts the wires, too."[3]

When people have multiple sclerosis, they really have a disease that has two distinct phases. First, the person with MS does not know something bad is happening. Nerves are being attacked and destroyed inside the body. The second part of MS is visible: The person feels pain and loss of function, and other people can easily see that the patient is having trouble seeing, walking, and talking.

MS is the name given to four distinct patterns of disease development. How the disease will affect the person differs with each form. How doctors treat the disease is also different for each form of the disease.

Relapsing Forms of MS

There are three types of relapsing MS. In relapsing MS, a person suffers a clear, acute flare-up of the disease (a relapse),

Depending on the form of the disease, a person with MS may have different symptoms. These two brothers both have multiple sclerosis. One is using a cane, and one is using a wheelchair.

with or without recovery of activity. Then, at some later time, the person will experience another relapse.

Relapsing-remitting MS. When a patient is first diagnosed with multiple sclerosis, the most common form of the disease is called relapsing-remitting MS. People can suffer an acute attack of the disease, such as the optic neuritis that Dylan Humphrey had. When that attack ends, there may be partial or complete recovery of vision. In between flare-ups, the disease does not get worse.

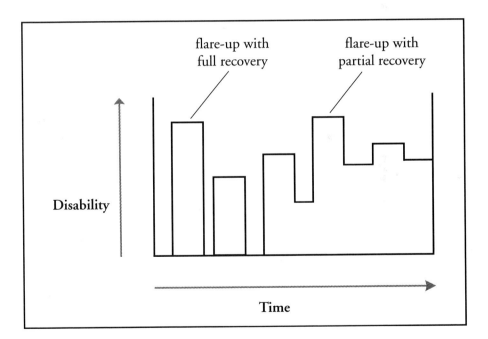

People with relapsing-remitting multiple sclerosis have clear flare-ups when disability increases (relapses). The flare-ups can be followed by a complete or partial recovery (remission).

Courtesy of the National Multiple Sclerosis Society.

Secondary-progressive MS. Within ten years of initial diagnosis, half the people with relapsing-remitting MS develop a form of MS called secondary-progressive MS.[4] In secondary-progressive MS, people first experience relapsing-remitting disease. Then, the disease steadily worsens, which may or may not include occasional flare-ups of the disease.

For example, say a person who could lift sixty pounds with one arm suffered an attack of MS that made that arm useless. After a time, strength would return, but now the person could only lift forty-five pounds. Then, after a second attack, the arm could only lift thirty-five pounds, and so on.

Although this example covers just weakness, there can be similar losses in vision, leg strength, or arm strength. It is also possible that there will be some loss of function in two or three different parts of the body at the same time.

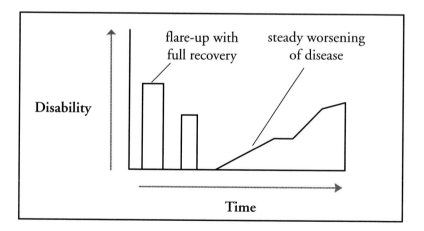

People with secondary-progressive multiple sclerosis first have relapsing-remitting MS. Then, they begin to get steadily worse. They may or may not have flare-ups during the worsening of the disease.
Courtesy of the National Multiple Sclerosis Society.

Progressive-relapsing MS. The third type of relapsing MS is progressive-relapsing MS. From the time they are diagnosed, people with progressive-relapsing MS show a steady decline in their ability to function. They also have very sharp attacks of the disease that can last for days or weeks. Once the acute attack is over, the condition returns to about the level it was before the attack. Then, the disease again progresses as more and more abilities are lost. Occasionally, after an acute attack subsides, patients may find that they can do more than before the attack. These improvements rarely last, and the progressive nature of the disease soon resumes, wiping out any improvement.

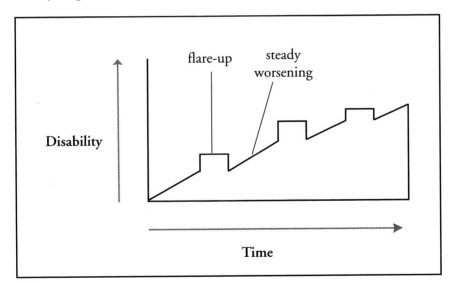

People with progressive-relapsing multiple sclerosis have a steady worsening of the disease from the time they are diagnosed. They also have clear flare-ups, with or without a return to their previous state. In between flare-ups, you can see that the disease continues to worsen.
Courtesy of the National Multiple Sclerosis Society.

37

At times, people who have a disease such as multiple sclerosis feel better. There are days in which a person can do things that he or she could not have done one or two or three months earlier. The improvements usually last for just a short time. Multiple sclerosis, especially the progressive forms of the disease, does not reverse course for an extended period.

Progressive MS

Betty Iams of San Diego was fifty-six years old—older than the usual person who contracts MS—when she began to experience weakness in her legs. Several health care professionals suggested that her problems were related to an old back injury. She continued her lifestyle until a year later.

> I noticed some sense of loss of balance and hyper-reflexes on my right side, as well as an increase in my right leg weakness and fatigue. I began a serious search to discover the source of my problem. It became increasingly difficult to continue my state of denial when my friends and associates were asking me why I was limping. My excuse of "new shoes" was getting weak.[5]

Eventually medical specialists diagnosed Iams as having primary-progressive multiple sclerosis. Progressive MS also has two main patterns.

In one pattern, a person's condition continually goes downhill from the time of diagnosis. The speed at which the decline continues differs from one person to another. There are no improvements, however, and the person may move from difficulty in walking to needing a cane, then a walker, then a wheelchair. Vision may become blurred, then more blurred and less and less useful. Overall function deteriorates.

In the other pattern of progressive MS, the course of the disease is also steadily downward from the time of diagnosis. However, there are variations in the rate of the disease progression, and there may be times when the progression stops or there are minor improvements. The condition may remain for months before another bout of MS leaves the person with less ability to move about. Sometimes, there can be limited improvements, but these improvements are wiped out in subsequent attacks of the disease.

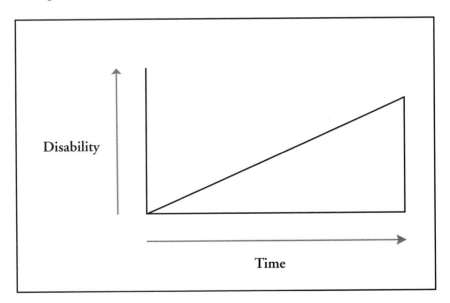

From the time of diagnosis, people with primary-progressive multiple sclerosis have almost a continuous worsening. There are no clear flare-ups. Sometimes, there are temporary small improvements.
Courtesy of the National Multiple Sclerosis Society.

Is MS Contagious?

Doctors believe that you cannot catch MS from another person. MS is not infectious. If you have a friend whose mother has MS, your friend cannot catch the disease from the parent. You cannot catch the disease from your friend. Multiple sclerosis is believed to be an immune-system disease.

The immune system in the body, when it is working normally, keeps a person healthy. Substances in the immune system can detect bacteria, viruses, or other foreign substances. When a foreign substance is detected, the immune system releases a series of chemicals, including antibodies, that find the foreign substance and destroy it.

For unknown reasons, sometimes the immune system becomes activated when there are no foreign bodies present. When that happens, the released antibodies attack healthy tissues. In MS, the immune system confuses the healthy myelin with another substance, perhaps a virus that may resemble substances that reside on the myelin. The immune-system antibodies then attack the myelin.

Another mechanism in development of MS occurs because the immune system fails to turn off when it is fighting another type of virus. More and more antibodies are produced. Those antibodies continue their search-and-destroy mission. However, there are no more bacteria or virus available to attack. Instead, myelin is attacked and damaged.

MS and Genetics

Some doctors think there is a genetic link to MS. Something in a person's genes—the basic building blocks of the body—may have some kind of error that could result in disease. It may also mean that nothing will ever happen. It may mean that a person is vulnerable to being affected by a virus or something toxic that is eaten or inhaled.

Most researchers of MS assume that the genetic error among people with MS causes no problems by itself. However, if a person with that genetic error picks up a certain virus, a reaction occurs that leads to MS. Right now we do not know what specific genetic error is the bad player in MS. We also do not know what virus or other insult to the body triggers the cascade of events leading to MS.[6]

MS is not inherited, however. It is not transmitted from one person to the next generation. So if a person's mother has MS, the children will not necessarily contract the disease. But there does appear to be some people who are more likely to get the disease in families where MS is present. That is known as genetic susceptibility to the disease.

Pam Iannello understood that she might have that genetic susceptibility to MS because two of her family members had the disease. Early in 1990, Iannello began experiencing blurred and double vision for several months, and was diagnosed as having MS.[7]

"I was always concerned in the back of my mind that I would someday develop MS. When I started having drastic

Researchers believe that MS is not contagious and cannot be inherited. If a parent has MS, it does not mean that the children will have MS.

vision problems, I knew what the prognosis would be," she said.

Iannello was able to continue working despite her vision problems. However, the disease forced her to give up her needlepoint hobby. MS has slowed her down, but has not stopped her from doing what she wants to do: raise her two children, continue to create stained glass, and learn how to fly a plane.

Although she knows that MS has a genetic link, she says she is not worried that her daughter will get MS. "If and when she is ever diagnosed with MS, I am confident that medical science will be so advanced that treating MS will be as routine and manageable as treating diabetes," she said. People with diabetes, another chronic disease, require daily injections of insulin, but they can live normally with the condition for decades.

Some Possible Risk Factors

There is an increased risk to children, brothers, and sisters of people with MS. The slightly increased risk to children may reflect not only something in the genes but something in the environment. Since families live together, eat similar things, go on similar vacations, and have similar pets, it is possible that a common element in their living environment is the trigger for the disease.

Recently researchers at the National Institute of Neurological Disorders and Stroke, an agency of the National Institutes of Health, run by the federal government, suggested that human herpesvirus 6 (HHV-6) might be involved in the MS process.

There are many herpesviruses. One type gives us cold sores on the lips; others cause shingles, painful itchy bumps on the skin; still other herpesviruses are responsible for chicken pox and a sexually transmitted disease called genital herpes.

New studies indicate that HHV-6 is associated with MS because the virus has been found in some patients with MS. In one study it was found circulating in the blood in fifteen of the fifty MS patients tested for the virus. The scientists also tested forty-seven other people who did not have MS, and none of them had HHV-6.[8]

Stephen Reingold of the National Multiple Sclerosis Society was cautious in interpreting the results of the study. He said, "This is evidence indicating it is a promising lead, but they have by no means demonstrated that [HHV-6] is a cause of MS or a trigger for MS."[9]

Herpes is not the first virus to be considered with MS. Dr. Randall Schapiro of the MS Education Network on the Internet says an outbreak of MS on some remote North

Vision Problems in MS[10]

Several vision problems are associated with multiple sclerosis:

- Optic neuritis, a condition that arises when inflammation occurs along the optic nerve. Optic neuritis usually affects just one eye and can result in temporary loss of vision, decreased vision, or blurred vision. Colors may appear washed out, and night vision may suffer.

- Central scotoma, occurrence of a blind spot in the center of vision.

- Nystagmus, involuntary movement of the eyeball. The eyeball may move up and/or down, often in jerky patterns.

- Diplopia, double vision caused by a failure of the eyes to coordinate well with each other.

Atlantic islands during World War II was first attributed to viruses. At the start of World War II there were many cases of MS in the Shetland and Orkney Islands north of Great Britain. Nearby are the Faroe Islands, which were occupied during World War II by British troops. Shortly after that occupation, there was an epidemic of MS in the Faroes. "We thought for years that viruses are involved in multiple sclerosis," Schapiro said, "but we've never been able to pin one down."[11]

Researchers thought that the virus that triggers MS might be a relative of the distemper virus. They theorized that the virus was carried by dogs that accompanied the troops stationed on the islands. In fact, researchers were not able to find a viral cause in the Faroe epidemic.

Schapiro said, "Every year or two somebody thinks they have found a viral cause of MS. A few years ago we though it was a retrovirus similar to AIDS but not the AIDS virus. It was called HTLV-1 virus. That's what it is still called, but it isn't the cause of multiple sclerosis. So until we can pin it down, we still have to just wonder whether there is a virus and what that virus is. We don't really know yet."[12]

4

Symptoms of Multiple Sclerosis

A t first, it was just numbness around my abdomen, like part of me had gone to sleep," says one man who described his first encounter with multiple sclerosis.[1] For Sir Augustus D'Este it was difficulty seeing.[2] The coaches and parents of high school basketball star Sarah Warnock spotted the fatigue in the sixteen-year-old athlete's steps.[3]

These are some ways multiple sclerosis first appears in people who contract the disease. The symptoms of MS vary from a vague tingling in the fingertips to an inability to use an arm, or from a slight blurriness in vision to near blindness. It is often difficult for both the person with MS and for doctors trying to diagnose the illness to document these signs of the disease. The symptoms of multiple sclerosis are also symptoms of other conditions.

Numbness and Tingling

People who suffer from multiple sclerosis frequently experience numbness or tingling in the fingers or elsewhere. The numbness has nothing to do with the fingers and feet being weakened, but it is caused by the failure of nerves to transmit signals from the feet, toes, and fingers to the brain. Numbness actually is the inability to feel sensations. There may also be tingling sensations as if a foot or arm has gone to sleep. Instead of lasting a few minutes, these sensations last for days.

There are several types of numbness and tingling that occur in MS patients. There is the feeling of pins and needles or a crawling sensation, as if an imaginary insect is walking on the skin. There can be a burning sensation that follows the path of a nerve. These sensations can change with touch or pressure. Even a light touch can produce a painful reaction. Finally, there is the complete loss of feeling in the fingers or toes. A person cannot feel touch, pain, or temperature.[4]

Vision Problems

People with multiple sclerosis often have blurred vision, double vision, or pain in moving an eyeball. These visual symptoms result from inflammation on nerves near the optic nerve—the main nerve that takes visual messages to the brain. When the inflammation goes away, so does double vision, blurred vision, or pain in moving the eyeball.

Fatigue

The most common symptom that people with MS have to cope with is fatigue. Fatigue is a normal condition for all of us that follows a full day of activities either at work, at home, or on vacation. However, when fatigue occurs to people with MS, it is overwhelming. For example, taking out a bag of garbage can be enough to leave a person exhausted for the rest of the day.

Fatigue in people with MS may be caused mainly by the slowing of nerve impulses. For reasons that are not fully understood, fatigue tends to worsen when a person is experiencing a

Some people with multiple sclerosis experience vision problems. Other symptoms include fatigue and dizziness.

stressful condition or participating in physical activities, or when a person is exposed to heat. Because the nerve impulses are slower, the person with MS has to concentrate harder than others to make their muscles do what is ordered by the brain. It can become mentally and physically tiring.

Because a person feels tired, he or she may then become frustrated. That frustration makes it more difficult to cope with the activities of everyday living.

Spasticity

In England recently, a driver with multiple sclerosis suffered a sudden leg spasm, causing his car to go out of control. The car struck several pedestrians, killing a person. Eventually the man was put on trial. Prosecutors claimed that because the driver had MS, he should not have been driving. However, thousands of people with MS can drive and need to drive in order to get around. A jury in the case found the man to be not guilty.[5]

The condition that occurred to the driver is known as spasticity, a condition that often befalls people with MS. When the signals from the brain to the arms and legs become disrupted, the muscles in the body fail to respond smoothly. Muscle tightness or spasms in muscles can result in people's arms and legs suddenly jerking to one side or another. Sometimes these spasms will cause serious falls. Spasticity in patients with MS is usually the result of changes in the flow of nerve impulses.

When muscles work properly, they work in opposite directions. That is, when one muscle flexes, the other relaxes. When both muscles pull or contract at the same time, spasticity occurs.[6] For example, a woman may want to move her arm to pick up a bottle of water, yet nothing happens. She tries harder to make that arm move, and this time the muscle reacts—but with too much force. The arm swings wildly and knocks the bottle off the table.

Tremors

Tremor is an involuntary shaking or trembling. When a person with MS has a "gross tremor," the shaking is very obvious. You can see a person's foot shaking back and forth as he or she tries to take a step.

Other people with MS have "fine tremor," an oscillation so slight that you might not notice anything. When a person with fine tremor picks up a glass containing liquid, you might see ripples appear on the surface or some liquid might splash out of the glass.

In MS, tremors vary in speed, severity, location, and duration. Tremors can affect the arms, legs, or head.

Tremors are caused by inflammation of nerves near the brain stem or the blockage of nerve signals between the brain stem and the cerebellum. The brain stem is located at the base of the brain and connects the brain with the spinal cord. The cerebellum is located just above the brain stem.

Speech Problems

Speech problems do not occur as frequently in people with MS as other symptoms. However, some of the speech patterns that do occur are almost exclusively related to MS.

One kind of speech disorder is known as dysarthria. People who develop dysarthria may have slurred speech. Their speech rhythm can be choppy.

Another speech problem is known as "scanning." This is a condition in which words are expressed in a jerky fashion. Scanning is usually only found in people with MS, whereas dysarthria can be an indication of several diseases.[7]

Bladder Control

Bladder problems often occur in patients with multiple sclerosis who suffer from scarring on their spinal cords. When the nerve messages along the spine are disrupted, muscles that control urination may relax. An unexpected relaxation of these muscles can mean that a person will leak urine. Some people may not be able to empty their bladders; other people may experience a need to urinate many times a day, including having to wake up in the middle of the night to go to the bathroom. The condition is called incontinence. Bladder-training techniques and some medications can help people with MS keep their bladder function working correctly; others will wear absorbent products such as diaperlike garments.

Dizziness

Many people with MS suffer from bouts of dizziness. They may also refer to the condition as light-headedness or loss of balance. More severe cases of dizziness are called vertigo.

Dizziness and vertigo, however, are frequently symptoms of many other conditions. For example, if you are playing outside on a very warm day and you become dehydrated—your body loses a lot of water through perspiration—you may feel dizzy. The condition can be associated with various medications. It also occurs when a person has an illness such as the flu.

When a person suffers vertigo, there is a feeling of movement with the light-headedness. In many cases people say they feel as if they are spinning, floating, or falling. Some people even have a combination of these sensations. Vertigo is often associated with problems that occur in the inner ear. In serious cases, patients with vertigo can become nauseous, and the condition can cause vomiting.

When dizziness occurs in people with MS, most often there is some form of inflammation that occurs near the brain stem. The brain stem controls many of our bodies' activities, such as eye coordination and balance.

Other Symptoms

There are other symptoms of the disease, too—people may not be able to have sexual relations, they may have paralysis in their arms or legs, or they may become confused or forgetful. They may have just one symptom, or they may experience a group of problems all at once.

Sixteen-year-old Sarah Warnock was a star on the best high school girl's basketball team in the nation. Her parents began

A National Multiple Sclerosis Society program called "MS Through the Eyes of a Child" included drawings by children. Nicole of Oceanside, California, included her grandmother in her drawing.

to notice that she was beginning to struggle during her basketball games. Sarah herself had noticed fatigue and coordination problems. When her fatigue continued, her parents searched for answers. A magnetic resonance image (MRI)—a picture of internal organs created with the use of magnets and computers—revealed white spots on her brain. These white spots seen in MRI scans are believed to indicate inflammatory activity or tissue scarring. The results from the MRI and other neurological tests helped the doctors confirm that Sarah had MS.

Within a few months, Sarah could not even catch a basketball. Her arms and legs tingled. She had bouts of dizziness, and her fatigue continued. Her face and body became swollen by steroids—the drugs that she took to treat the attack. Her right hand became too weak to take notes in class, so she learned to write with her left hand. Double vision forced her to wear special glasses or an eye patch. Her legs stopped working, and she needed a wheelchair. She spent the days asleep on the couch at home. Her speech was slurred when she pleaded with her basketball coach, "Don't give up on me. I'm going to play basketball again."[8]

MS came close to destroying Sarah, but after spending months disabled, sometimes in a wheelchair, she was able to regain enough strength to go out and compete again at a top level. One year after her diagnosis, Sarah scored the winning point in a national tournament game.[9]

Remission

One consistent thing about multiple sclerosis is that it is a disease with symptoms difficult to predict. Patients may find that they can again move their legs, their vision and speech clear up, and their fatigue disappears.

This improvement in a patient's condition is known as a remission. Today, Sarah Warnock continues to battle MS, but the attacks seem to be less severe and are not holding her back. Her mother, Shirlene Warnock, says Sarah walks a little funny, but she is strong enough to play on the varsity basketball and track teams at Lewis and Clark College in Oregon. "Never say die," Sarah says in describing her fight against the disease. "I have MS. MS does not have me."[10]

Sarah has been diagnosed as having the relapsing-remitting form of MS. She is taking Avonex®, one of the three approved medicines that has shown some ability to control the disease. With the type of MS Sarah has, no one can tell when the next attack will be or how severe it will be. She continues to have five to six attacks each year, but she keeps coming back.

Michele Overgard is always aware that MS is with her, or as she refers to the disease as "it." "It" is a numbness in her hand and an itchy feeling in her palm. She can go ahead and do her daily work with "it," but every now and then "it" becomes an attack. Overgard, a writer, described the attacks in this way: "It creeps through my body, sometimes attaching itself to a specific tendon or muscle. Occasionally it starts with a burning sensation and evolves into an itch. Sometimes it

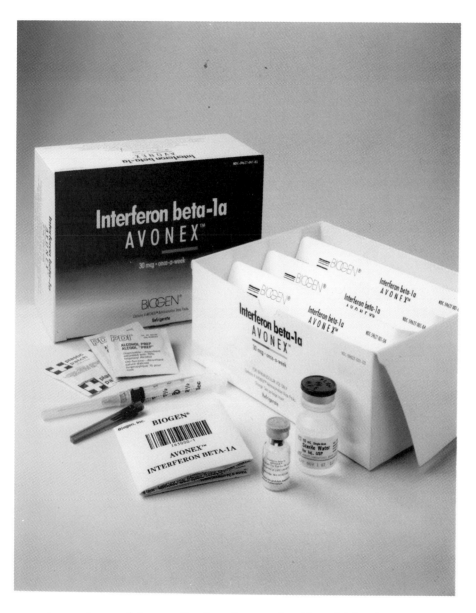

Avonex is one of three medications that people with multiple sclerosis use to control the disease.

stays confined to one area, but this time it couldn't make up its mind."[11]

In the space of a few hours, Overgrad's hands grew weak—time to break out the plastic glasses, she realized. Her left leg felt so heavy she had to grab at the fenders of cars to walk through her housing complex parking lot. Fatigue overcame her. Making things worse was the fact that her husband was out of town on business for a week. She was on her own, and wanted to prove to herself she could handle an MS attack by herself. She responded by taking medications and drinking fluids. The attack finally eased.

"I know 'it' may come back for another visit, but I'm not going to worry about it. I won over the fear factor. Who says we can't be home alone?"[12]

5

Diagnosis of Multiple Sclerosis

Although scientists and doctors have studied multiple sclerosis for more than a century, medical experts still have difficulty diagnosing the disease.

The first symptom of MS may be subtle, such as a transient vision problem or sudden weakness that disappears after a day or so. A second symptom might not occur for months. Therefore, patients often delay going to a doctor. By the time the patient sees the doctor, the symptom may have disappeared, giving the doctor little to examine, aside from the patient's own description. Frequently, several years pass between the time of the first symptoms and diagnosis.

There are characteristics of MS that make diagnosis easier for the doctor:

- The wide variety of symptoms—visual problems, paralysis, fatigue, hearing, and speech difficulties—indicates that the patient has damage to the nerves or brain stem.[1]

- Multiple lesions or plaques that are interrupting brain and nerve signals in the body will be evident.

- The course of the disease will follow a pattern of acute attack, followed by remission, followed by relapses. The French scientist Jean-Martin Charcot who created the name for MS was one of the first researchers to recognize the pattern of remission-relapse in MS.

- The reappearance of symptoms—such as leg weakness—in the same limb will occur. Even though other symptoms will occur, a hallmark of MS is that symptoms will return. Dylan Humphrey, for example, had recurrence with optic neuritis. Michele Overgard had previously experienced leg weakness and fatigue.

Even though there are a lot of signs pointing to MS, almost all the symptoms can be caused by numerous other diseases. Doctors will first eliminate other illnesses before diagnosing multiple sclerosis.

The Patient Can Help with Diagnosis

In trying to make a diagnosis, the doctor can be helped by the patient. Because many patients do not see a doctor when some of the symptoms occur, the doctor has to rely on a patient's memory. Betty Iams went to see her doctor when she had leg

MS Misdiagnosed in Women[2]

The fleeting symptoms of multiple sclerosis have always made it a difficult disease to diagnose. Many patients have experienced years of being shuttled from doctor to doctor without getting an accurate diagnosis. In fact, until the 1920s it was assumed that men suffered from multiple sclerosis more than women. Today it is known that women are more than twice as likely as men to contract multiple sclerosis. But in the early part of this century, women who complained of dizziness, weakness, vision problems, or other symptoms of MS were mistakenly diagnosed with "hysteria."

weakness. However, she now thinks her first MS symptoms occurred years earlier when she began to suffer minor bouts of incontinence, a loss of bladder control.

Diaries kept by Sir Augustus D'Este in the 1820s and Dylan Humphrey in the 1990s are important because they can help doctors develop an accurate history of the patient's disease. MS patients and those suspected of having MS are encouraged to keep diaries of the illness to help doctors diagnose and treat the disease.

Sometimes a patient will undergo a period in which his or her hands are numb. By itself, that does not mean the person has MS. Another time a person may feel weak or suffer from fatigue for no apparent reason. Even taken together that does not mean a person has MS.

However, when there are a number of symptoms that seem to occur and then disappear, a doctor may become suspicious that MS is the cause of these various complaints.

Typically, the doctor will review the history of the symptoms to see whether those symptoms are similar to those known to be involved with MS. In addition, the doctor will perform a neurological examination to test a patient's reflexes, vision, strength, and coordination. An abnormal result could show that nerve impulses are taking longer than expected. Perhaps MS is the cause.

The doctor will also perform tests on sensations—how a person responds to sense of touch, sight, hearing, smell, and pain. Again the purpose is to see whether there is something altering a normal response.[3]

If doctors believe that a patient has a neurological disorder and suspect MS, they may order a magnetic resonance imaging (MRI) scan of the brain or spinal cord.

Because an MRI is expensive, doctors are reluctant to order the tests unless they are confident that the result will help support a definitive diagnosis.

"MS remains very much a disease that is diagnosed by eliminating other illnesses," said Dr. Stephen Reingold. "Even an MRI scan cannot give a definitive diagnosis of MS."[4] However, MS remains a clinically diagnosed disease based on a person's history, examination, and laboratory findings.

An MRI scan is created by a sophisticated diagnostic machine. In performing an MRI scan, a patient lies enclosed within a tubelike cylinder between an array of powerful magnets.

A doctor will discuss a patient's symptoms with her to help in the diagnosis of multiple sclerosis.

When the magnetic field of the MRI is activated, invisible radio waves are aimed at the body. The radio waves create a signal in the cells of the body. A computer calculates how the nuclei of the cells react to the radio waves. The computer then uses this electronic information to produce a picture. That picture becomes an illustration of the inside of a person's body. If a person has multiple sclerosis, the MRI will typically illustrate evidence of disease in the form of white spots in the brain.

If the history, neurological examinations, and MRI results indicate that MS may be the cause of the various symptoms that the patient suffers, a doctor may then order an examination of spinal fluid. A needle is used in a spinal tap to puncture the spinal canal and a small amount of fluid is examined under the microscope. The doctor is searching for evidence of proteins or banding of proteins that may support the diagnosis. Other diseases, such as Lyme disease, can then be eliminated.

Even if a patient is suffering from symptoms associated with MS, has positive neurological and MRI examinations, and if the spinal fluid tests show suspicious results, a diagnosis of MS is still made indirectly by the doctor.[5]

Dr. J.H.D. Millar, a neurologist at Royal Victoria Hospital at The Queen's University in Belfast, Northern Ireland, said, "It is inadvisable to tell the patient he or she has multiple sclerosis before a firm diagnosis is made, as the label tends to stick, and the possibility of an alternative diagnosis may be overlooked."[6]

6

Treatment of Multiple Sclerosis

For most of the history of multiple sclerosis, the options doctors and patients faced involved only how to treat the symptoms of the disease. Until 1993 there were no medications that actually succeeded in reducing the number of MS attacks or the severity of those flare-ups.

Over the years, however, doctors have been able to find numerous treatments for the symptoms as they arose. A number of those treatments do not involve drugs. Often, the symptoms can be relieved by learning how to live with the disease.

For example, one woman, Nancy, was diagnosed with multiple sclerosis when she was in her twenties. She has lived with relapsing multiple sclerosis for more than a decade.[1]

She and her husband are building a home—a home designed to allow a person with MS to function as normally and as efficiently as possible. In their new home, the doors of all the rooms are extrawide. If MS continues to reduce Nancy's ability to walk, the wider doors will allow easier use of a wheelchair. The bathroom and kitchen drawers are at lower levels so someone in a wheelchair has easier access. Nancy has decided that having a disease will not prohibit her from preparing meals or sacrificing her personal independence because she cannot reach certain items. The edges of sinks, tables, and counters are padded to prevent injuries that might occur if a sudden MS attack causes loss of balance or muscle spasms.

Nancy is prepared for the disease. However, medications are still going to be necessary to handle the flare-ups when they occur. For example, if vision problems caused by swelling and irritation around the optic nerves occur, doctors may prescribe steroids to control the inflammation. If itching develops as a symptom of MS, drugs that could be rubbed on the skin may be offered to patients.

Treating the Symptoms

NUMBNESS AND TINGLING

There are not any medications to specifically treat numbness. Many experts do not believe treatment is necessary because there really is nothing wrong with the fingers and toes. What

Some changes in the home can make daily life easier for someone who has multiple sclerosis.

is wrong is the ability of the nerves to transmit signals between the spinal cord or the brain and the fingers and toes.

Instead of drugs, many patients simply try to ignore the symptom and concentrate on other matters. Only in the most difficult cases, where numbness or tingling are interfering with normal activity, are medications prescribed.[2]

Doctors will rarely prescribe steroids for treatment of numbness and tingling because these symptoms do not interfere with function. Cortisone, a steroid, reduces inflammation around the nerves, and that may help increase feeling. Many doctors would rather avoid steroids for numbness.[3] Other more serious conditions also require steroids, and overuse might reduce the drugs' effectiveness. Also, a side effect of chronic steroid use is cataracts. Cataracts cause cloudy vision and sometimes need to be surgically removed.

Doctors have reported some success in using antiseizure drugs to control painful burning sensations. Tranquilizers may also reduce numbness.

VISION PROBLEMS

Vision problems often go away without any medication. The problems arise due to inflammation, and when the inflammation goes away, so does double vision, blurred vision, or pain in moving the eyeball. Nystagmus, a condition of involuntary eyeball movement that has been associated with MS for more than one hundred years, also may disappear without treatment in some cases.[4] Steroids reduce inflammation and may result in full or partial improvement.

The jerky eye movements of nystagmus can also be treated with an eye patch or with certain tranquilizers.

FATIGUE

Doctors say that the best way to combat the fatigue of MS is to change a person's lifestyle to reduce physical activity. However, reducing physical activity does not mean a person should stop exercising. Exercise is important in maintaining muscle tone and other body functions. A person should not, however, exercise to the point that he or she becomes fatigued.

People with MS who have fatigue as a symptom of their disease should plan ahead. By knowing what is most important in the day, the person can complete priorities early in the day, and save the less urgent tasks until the next day or until the symptom passes.

People such as Nancy can use adaptive furniture or kitchen appliances to help with work in the home. People should look for objects that roll, rather than have to be pushed; objects that slide, rather than have to be carried.

When medication is needed for fatigue, doctors will often prescribe amantadine. Amantadine helps release dopamine, a substance in the brain that helps communication between cells. Fatigue in MS patients is mainly caused by the slowing of nerve impulses. Amantadine may help speed these messages. Other medications used are stimulants or antidepressants such as Prozac®.[5]

SPASTICITY

Spasticity is one of the most common symptoms of MS, and it is also one of the most distressing. Patients can be performing

Exercise is an important activity to maintain muscle tone in people with multiple sclerosis.

normal tasks when their muscles suddenly refuse to work together or become tight or painful. Typical treatments to combat spasticity include exercise, physical therapy, and medications.

People who suffer from these spasms are encouraged to stretch muscles and muscle groups, sometimes in a pool where the buoyancy of the water makes it possible to work the muscles while using less energy.

There are medications that can help overcome the spasms. These relaxant drugs, however, can make a person feel sleepy. In some cases with small muscle groups, doctors have been successful in using a tiny amount of a poison that results in the food poisoning known as botulism. The poison is called botulin. When a person eats food contaminated with botulin, the muscles of the body become paralyzed, and death can follow in minutes. In MS, tiny amounts of this same poison can control muscles that are uncontrolled in other methods.[6]

Other medications are also helpful. Baclofen® and Zanaflexane® are often prescribed because they reduce spasticity. The drugs have to be carefully monitored by doctors because too much can cause muscle weakness; too little is ineffective. Tranquilizers can also be used, especially for people who suffer spasticity at night.

TREMOR

Tremor is one of the most difficult multiple sclerosis symptoms to treat. A tremor is also difficult to live with. Sometimes, balance and coordination exercises are used to help a person compensate for the tremor. Sometimes weights are added to the ankle or the wrist to decrease the movement during a tremor.

Medications can help minimally with tremors. Tranquilizers that calm patients can be helpful because tremors can be made worse by stress or anxiety. Drugs used to prevent spasticity may also help tremors.[7]

SPEECH PROBLEMS

Speech problems in people with MS are less common than other symptoms but do occur in some patients. If speech problems persist for more than a couple of months, patients should consult with a speech therapist.

Mouth exercises can help patients with enunciation. Some of those exercises include exaggerating speech. The exaggeration slows speech down, which makes it possible to form words that are more clearly understood.

In severe cases of speech abnormalities in MS, a person may learn to use a communications board that has series of letters, words, and pictures that can help a person communicate with others without speaking.

BLADDER CONTROL

For MS patients with bladder control problems, the psychological effects of not having control of their bladders are usually more difficult than the occasional urine leakage.

Patients can take medications to control spastic bladder. These drugs block reflexes in the bladder, giving the patient more control over when to empty the bladder. Absorbent clothing can be worn to soak up any accidental leakage.

Can I Inherit MS?[8]

In general, the chance of anyone developing MS is about one in one thousand. For example, in a city of twenty thousand people, there may be twenty people who get multiple sclerosis. If a parent has MS, the risk to a child rises to 2 percent for boys and 3 percent for girls. That means for every one hundred parents with MS, two to three of their children will get the disease. Although people do not directly inherit MS, it appears that they do inherit the ability to get MS. In addition to inheriting the ability to get the disease, something else must happen for the disease to emerge. As of now, no one is sure what that something else is.

However, says Dr. Randall Schapiro, director of the Fairview Multiple Sclerosis Center in Minneapolis, Minnesota, "Because inheritance has so little influence on MS, it is not something to be overly concerned about." He said that a small risk should not influence a person's decision about whether to have children of their own.

Many people believe that MS runs in families, but only in one family in five can someone with MS find another relative with the disease.

In some cases, patients can empty their bladder with a catheter, a thin tube that is inserted through the urethra and up the urinary tract into the bladder. The catheter allows urine to flow down the tube into a plastic bag in a safe, controlled manner. Although it sounds difficult, people with MS can perform the catheter insertion easily and rapidly, even in a bathroom stall at a shopping mall, theater, or restaurant.

Bladder infections may occur in MS patients. These infections can be prevented, sometimes just by drinking cranberry juice, taking vitamin C, or by emptying the bladder frequently. These juices make urine acidic, a condition that can suppress bacteria in the bladder. Drinking a lot of fluids—water and juices—also flushes the urinary system of harmful infection-causing organisms.[9]

Treating MS Attacks

Since 1993 there has been a revolution in the treatment of multiple sclerosis. Until this point, doctors treated the disease symptoms when the inevitable flare-ups occurred. Doctors can now treat the illness directly, influencing the course of MS for the first time.

The three medications that have created this revolution are Betaseron®, Avonex®, and Copaxone®. These therapies have shown they can reduce the severity, duration, and number of exacerbations—acute attacks of MS. None of the drugs claims to eliminate the attacks altogether or change the course of the disease.

Betaseron and Avonex are beta-interferons. Interferons are proteins produced naturally by the body. Interferons help fight viral infections and help regulate the immune system. No one knows exactly how the interferons work in multiple sclerosis. It is believed they decrease the body's destructive immune response against myelin, the fatty insulation surrounding nerve fibers.

Copaxone is a man-made polymer. Its use for treating MS came about when scientists in Israel noticed that laboratory animals injected with the polymer did not come down with a disease similar to MS. As with the interferons, exactly why Copaxone works in MS is unknown. However, scientists believe that Copaxone modifies the immune processes that are now believed to cause MS.

All the drugs have to be administered through injection. If the drugs were given orally as pills, their active ingredients would be digested by the stomach before they could help in reducing MS attacks.

Betaseron: The First of the New Drugs

In 1993 the Food and Drug Administration (FDA) approved the first drug that was specifically indicated for multiple sclerosis, interferon beta-1b, which is marketed under the trade name of Betaseron. It is given by injections under the skin. The injections have to be taken every other day. Betaseron has been shown to be effective in reducing the number of MS attacks. The reduction is impressive, but it does not eliminate the attacks.

75

After years of studying the effects of this drug on MS patients, doctors concluded that patients with the relapsing-remitting form of MS could take Betaseron for long periods. Betaseron was shown to slow the rate of the number of relapses and decrease the severity of the relapses when they occurred. Further studies of Betaseron showed that people could take Betaseron and achieve reductions in MS attacks for five years or longer.[10]

The initial study of Betaseron performance found that patients taking the drug had 34 percent fewer relapses than people who were taking placebo medication by injection. Placebos look like the medication but contain no active ingredients. A 34 percent reduction means that if a patient was having an MS attack six times a year, then by taking the drug, the attacks would only occur about four times a year. People taking the drug also reported that the attacks did not seem to last as long and were not as severe as before they were taking the drug. For example, once Sarah Warnock began taking the medicines to try and control MS, the episodes that did occur lasted a few days instead of weeks.

Side Effects of Betaseron

Some people who take Betaseron experience side effects. They get tired and feverish and generally feel bad. However, doctors know that nonsteroidal anti-inflammatory drugs (NSAIDS) or Tylenol® can treat these symptoms. This reaction may be caused by the introduction of Betaseron, an interferon, to the body. When interferons increase in the body, there is a reaction among other cells that can make a person feel as if he or she is suffering from the flu. It is the result of the drug influencing other cells to fight off infections. Because some scientists believe that a virus is at work in MS, the virus-fighting power of the interferons apparently helps reduce the MS attacks.

Other patients taking Betaseron also have pain or soreness at the place where the injection takes place, although these inflammations or "site reactions" decrease in severity as the patients use Betaseron.

Betaseron causes some changes in liver functions and some blood cell abnormalities. Regular tests are required to make sure that these problems do not threaten the patient. Doctors

New Drugs Are Expensive

A comparative survey by the National Multiple Sclerosis Society estimates that

- A year's supply of Betaseron will cost between $11,000 and $13,000.
- For Avonex, the cost is estimated to be $11,000 a year.
- Copaxone is expected to cost about $10,000 a year.
- Health insurance often picks up the bulk of the cost.
- There are support programs offered by each manufacturer to help patients obtain treatment.

will draw blood from the patient taking Betaseron and have it analyzed in laboratories.

Sometimes patients who are taking Betaseron will develop proteins in the blood called neutralizing antibodies. These antibodies might act against the drug and reduce the ability of Betaseron to work against MS.[11]

Avonex: Another Drug for the Arsenal

In May 1996 the FDA approved another drug for multiple sclerosis, interferon beta-1a, marketed under the trade name of Avonex. Avonex is the drug that Roger Kennedy of West Virginia began using when doctors were finally able to diagnose his illness.

When government regulators approved Avonex, it was made available to treat patients who have relapsing-remitting multiple sclerosis.[12]

The approval was based on results from trials with men and women that suggested the drug slowed down the progression of physical disability of people with MS. The studies also showed that Avonex reduced the number of relapses or flare-ups of MS. Patients on Avonex also experienced an 18 percent reduction in the frequency of flare-ups of the symptoms. The reduction in frequency of flare-ups is similar to that seen with Betaseron.

Whereas Betaseron is taken by injection under the skin every other day, Avonex is injected into the muscle once a week. Sometimes the injection is given by a nurse or a doctor in their office, but some patients can learn how to give themselves the injections so they do not have to plan vacations or other activities around doctors appointments.

Patients taking Avonex report the side effects of treatment to be short-term flulike symptoms—fever, chills, muscle aches, and fatigue. But symptoms vary with patients. Patients can avoid or reduce the side effects by taking NSAIDs or Tylenol just prior to injection.

Some patients on Avonex come down with mild cases of anemia. Anemia is a lower than normal level of cells in the blood that carry oxygen. People with anemia can look pale and sometimes feel weak.

Patients with MS might switch from one drug to another to try and find the one that helps them the most, yet causes the least discomfort in their lives. Advice from health care practitioners is needed to make those decisions.

"JG," a thirty-three-year-old mother of two children, had been experiencing exacerbation of the disease once or twice a month since she was twenty-five. JG learned about Betaseron on the Internet, got on the waiting list, and then began using the drug when it became available.

JG found that taking Betaseron resulted in flulike symptoms—a common side effect when taking interferon drugs. When the newer product—the once weekly drug Avonex was available—JG chose to switch. With the new medication plan, she had no flulike symptoms.

This time, her health care practitioner told her how to minimize side effects by taking the drug in the evening along with a couple of Tylenol tablets.

The pharmacist and the patient talked about goals for this therapy. The pharmacist cautioned her not to expect complete remission of the MS. They also spent time discussing realistic goals for therapy, financial reimbursement plans, and follow-up conferences.

On the new drug, JG is happier. More important, she takes the medication the way it is prescribed, which gives her the best chance of reducing MS attacks. With proper training and discussions with health care providers, most people who take the medications can have the same success that JG had.[13]

Copaxone: Another Mode of Action

In 1993, Melissa Hawkins-Holt, a college student with dreams of becoming a doctor, suddenly developed bouts of numbness in her hands and feet. Her vision was sometimes blurred. Finally the problems became bad enough to interfere with her life. She went to a hospital for an explanation.

The diagnosis was multiple sclerosis. Hawkins-Holt decided to enter a clinical trial of an experimental new drug called glatiramer acetate. Glatiramer acetate was being used to protect people with MS from further attacks of the disease. The drug is administered by daily injections under the skin.[14]

After several years of testing glatiramer acetate in animals and then in human beings, the U.S. Food and Drug Administration approved it for use in multiple sclerosis on December 23, 1996. The approval arrived just in time for the holiday season. Arney Rosenblat of the National Multiple

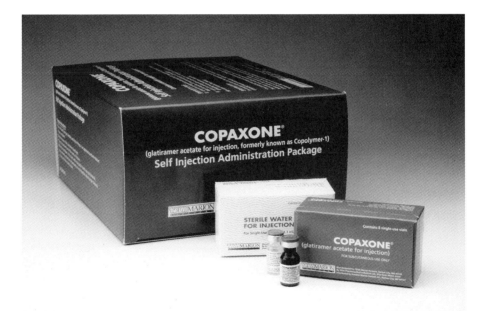

Copaxone has been approved to treat multiple sclerosis.

Sclerosis Society said, "This is a marvelous holiday gift for people with multiple sclerosis."

Copaxone has the scientific name of glatiramer acetate, but almost everyone refers to it as Copaxone.[15] Copaxone differs from the other two drugs, Betaseron and Avonex, in that it is not an interferon-based product. It does not create the flulike symptoms that often accompany interferon injections.

Copaxone is refrigerated, as are the interferons, until ready for use, when patients add sterile water to prepare the injection. It is distributed through pharmacies or it can also be delivered directly to the patient.

"Copaxone is well tolerated with no clinically significant difference in flulike symptoms, depression, or fatigue when compared to placebo, unlike other MS therapies," says Kenneth Johnson, M.D., of the University of Maryland Medical Center in Baltimore, a principal investigator of clinical trials with Copaxone.

Scientists have looked for neutralizing antibodies in patients that take Copaxone, but have not found that the drug causes production of these proteins.

In March 1998, Johnson reported that after almost three years of taking Copaxone there was a 32 percent reduction in the number of MS-like attacks.[16] Johnson said, "Each relapse can damage the nervous system and increase the likelihood of disability." When the research team used scientific measurements to determine how much disability was involved, they determined that people taking Copaxone were 50 percent less likely to be disabled than people who were not taking any medication.

The new medicine allowed Melissa Hawkins-Holt—now Dr. Hawkins-Holt—to complete college and medical school.

"I haven't had a significant relapse since I have been taking Copaxone," she said. "It makes me feel like I am doing something to give myself the best chance of remaining relapse-free as long as possible."[17]

7

MS Can Hurt Those Who Do Not Have It

When I was about nine, Mom came to my soccer game in her wheelchair. Some kid said, 'Who's the kooky lady in the wheelchair?' and I pretended I didn't know. Later I asked my mom not to come to the games anymore. I feel bad about that now, because I know it hurt her."[1]

Because multiple sclerosis usually strikes men and women in their twenties and thirties, the children who are as young as four or five suddenly find that they need to help take care of their parents. These children have to bring clothes to their parents, answer the telephone, even assist in preparing meals. The trips to the dance studio or Little League games that other children take for granted are no longer guaranteed for these children.

The impact of multiple sclerosis extends far beyond the person who has the disease. It affects those who have to care, watch, help, and encourage. The disease can interrupt and devastate family life and can play havoc with typical family roles.

The playmates of a child whose parent has MS may not understand what is going on. Because MS attacks can occur without warning at the worst possible time, children may find that their plans for parties, hiking trips, or attendance at ball games are suddenly canceled. Children are reluctant to tell playmates their parent has a disease that is hard to pronounce and even harder to explain.

Nicole Bagdriwicz from Sunnyvale, California, knows what it is like. "My mother was diagnosed with MS in 1989 when I was seven years old. I didn't understand what was wrong. I just knew Mom wasn't going to work anymore and she was always home to be with me. Telling my friends that Mom has MS is easy, but I'm embarrassed when I have to explain what it is and what it might do to her."

"My mom has MS," said Tiffany Rein, a thirteen-year-old from Amarillo, Texas.

> Most of the time things are pretty normal. But sometimes my mom struggles with MS and even though she tried not to let it show, we know she doesn't feel good.
>
> I think what is most difficult for me is when we choose things to do on family days, I always want her to be part of it. We try to pick things we can all do. Some families go skating or they ride bikes together and stuff like that to have fun. But when we do these things my mom only watches.

Tiffany won national recognition by drawing a picture of what MS looks like to her. Her drawing shows a woman in a cage, chains around her hands and feet. A man outside the cage holds keys. Tiffany explained, "The cage represents the world of MS—trapped in pain and confusion. The chains represent how MS restricts the choices people with this illness have. The locks represent how much control MS has in our life. The man represents the cure for MS. The keys represent hope."[2]

Helping Mom Make It Through the Day

Melissa Hinkes of Miami, Florida, is nine years old. She has always known that her mother has MS and that her role is to help her mother make it through the day.

> My mom has MS. Some days she just really can't take it. My mom is not in a wheelchair yet, and I hope she won't be. My mom got diagnosed when my little brother was three months old. Now my brother is seven. Every day I help my mother with her MS. Whenever she goes somewhere people look at her funny. And I know how it feels. I am nine, the middle child. It seems hard to have MS and three kids at the same time. . . .[3]

Shirlene Warnock whose daughter, while a member of the championship Oregon City High School basketball team was diagnosed with multiple sclerosis (see Chapter 4), said, "I get some heartbreaking telephone calls from children who have parents with multiple sclerosis or from parents who have the disease and are not sure how this affects their children."[4]

Tiffany's drawing shows what MS looks like to her.

"This is a terrible disease for children who have MS and for children whose loved ones have MS," Warnock said. She said it is easy for a friend to slip and say something bad about people or make a joke about someone in a wheelchair, forgetting for the moment that a friend has a parent at home in a wheelchair.

Having Someone to Talk To

As bad as having the disease or having a parent with the disease is the feeling that no one knows how you feel and that you have no one to talk to. The National Multiple Sclerosis Society suggests that children whose parents have MS should seek out someone they can talk to about what it is like to deal with MS in the family. Sometimes it is difficult to find a friend to talk to because friends may not have the experience of dealing with someone who has disabilities. A relative, sibling, teacher, clergyman, or the healthy parent may then be the person to turn to.[5]

It is also important for the child whose parent has MS to find out information about the disease. There are books in the school library and pamphlets from organizations that offer help to people with MS. (Some resources are listed in the For More Information section at the back of this book.)

Friends of children who have to help their parents deal with MS should also try to find out as much as possible about the disease so they can be good listeners for their friends. They should know something about MS if they are going to be able to understand why a friend has to rush home from school when he or she should be playing baseball instead.

Sometimes children need to help with family tasks. It can make the day easier for the parent with MS.

Famous People with MS

Multiple sclerosis can strike anyone. Some of the people include those from the world of entertainment, politics, and other fields.

Barbara Jordan, former United States congresswoman from Texas, was selected by *Time* magazine as one of the "Ten Women of the Year" in 1976. She died of viral pneumonia, a complication of leukemia, on January 17, 1996, in Austin, Texas. She was fifty-nine.[6]

Richard Pryor is a comedian and actor. In his most recent performances on-screen, Pryor acted in a wheelchair.[7]

Annette Funicello is the most famous and most loved of the actors and actresses who were part of "The Mickey Mouse Club" in the 1950s and 1960s. She also recorded hit songs and appeared in numerous movies.[8]

Clay Walker was one of the top country-and-western singers when he was diagnosed with multiple sclerosis at the age of twenty-seven.[9]

Joseph Hartzler is the federal prosecutor who secured a conviction against the man accused of blowing up the federal building in Oklahoma City in 1995, a crime that resulted in the deaths of 168 people. Hartzler often arrived at court in a motorized scooter or pleaded to the jury from a wheelchair.[10]

Alan Osmond is the oldest performing member of the family of singers that includes Donny and Marie Osmond. "Big Al," born in 1949, was diagnosed with MS after he fell while hiking with his family in 1996.[11]

Nicole Ketchum, fifteen, of Fair Oaks, California, knows what facing the truth is about when it comes to MS and how the disease affects her mother.

> I will never be ready to deal with the fact that my mother is going to get worse, that one day she may get in her wheelchair and never walk again. But when that day comes, when I look at my mother's face and see the tired worn-out look on it that always appears when she isn't well, I know that I won't deny it. I love my mother so much, she deserves for me to be brave and to face her and her disease. Even though I am scared, I will face and deal with the problem.[12]

8

A Future Without Multiple Sclerosis?

Scientists continue to investigate the reasons that multiple sclerosis creates damage in the brain and in the nervous system. The answers will tell them what causes the disease. Once the cause is known there may be ways researchers can find to stop the progress—and maybe even reverse the disease.

More and more scientists are finding out that whatever happens in the body, happens because genes do something. All disease, in some manner, has a genetic basis. Even if you catch a cold, the severity of your cold is regulated to some extent by how your genes create responses to certain viruses.

Genes are the instruction book for the body. In every cell in the body, there is a copy of a person's DNA. The DNA strand contains all the genes in the body in a set of structures known as chromosomes. In every human being there are billions of chemicals that have to function correctly to produce a healthy person. When all these chemical units and proteins work correctly, there is normal body function.

However, any number of things can go wrong. When cells reproduce, they make copies of the DNA. If the moment that a cell is replicating itself it is struck by radiation, or a toxin from something we eat or drink is present or some bacteria or virus is present, the DNA replication may be altered. In addition to the environmental damage to genes, the genes that we acquire from our parents can be faulty. The result can be an inherited genetic flaw. Scientists believe that in many diseases, including MS, people have to inherit certain genes and then have those genes activated by something in the environment.

Scientists around the world are working to unravel the human genome. When this Human Genome Project is completed, genetic specialists will know what every normal gene is supposed to look like. However, this "map" of genes is not the whole story. We will not necessarily know what these genes do. We will not know how the genes do what they are supposed to do. Scientists will look for abnormal genes in the bodies of people who have multiple sclerosis, rheumatoid arthritis, cancer, diabetes, and other chronic diseases in an attempt to find out what makes those genes work properly and what happens when those genes do not work correctly.

Even now, before the genome project has been completed, scientists have pinpointed nineteen different genes that they believe play a role in the development of multiple sclerosis. As yet, they do not know exactly how these nineteen genes figure in development of MS. There are rules to the genetic instructions. The only problem is that human beings do not know how those rules work. When we fully understand our bodies' building blocks—the genes—then we will begin to be able to do something about the errors that occur in the rules and correct them.

By understanding the genetic system, doctors should better understand what causes multiple sclerosis. They will be able to develop new ways of treating it and identify people who are at risk of developing the disease. Treatments can then begin even before there are symptoms—preventing the disease from ever occurring.[1]

Searching for a Virus

In addition to understanding the genetics of multiple sclerosis, research continues into trying to figure out what makes the body's immune system go haywire and start attacking its own healthy tissues, especially the important tissues of the brain and nervous system. For some reason, the mechanisms of defense in the body—that system that seeks out and destroys invaders such as bacteria and viruses—stop being able to distinguish between good tissue and bad tissue. It would not be possible for science to wipe out the immune system that attacks healthy cells because by doing that it could leave the body defenseless against unhealthy cells such as some bacteria. Somehow researchers will have to find a way to make the body's cells act properly in their defense job.

Among the groups that are actively seeking answers to multiple sclerosis are the National Institute for Neurological Disorders and Stroke (NINDS). NINDS spends more money on research for MS than any other organization. NINDS is one of the branches of the National Institutes of Health in Bethesda, Maryland. The National Multiple Sclerosis Society provides more research money than any other private group.

In the search for a cure for MS, researchers are focused on the search for a viral trigger for MS. If the theory that certain people are genetically predisposed to MS is correct, a relatively common virus might trigger the reaction that causes the MS process. Many researchers believe herpesvirus-6 could play a role in the MS trigger for some people. Most people have been exposed to herpesvirus-6. In children it causes roseola—a rash that occurs in response to fever. Researchers have noticed that during MS attacks, there seems to be an activation of herpesvirus-6. Scientists, however, are not sure if herpesvirus-6 actually triggers multiple sclerosis attacks or if it is just present in the body and becomes activated when something else triggers an MS attack. Herpesvirus-6 may lie dormant until some other trigger kicks it into gear.[2]

Attempts to Make Myelin Grow

Myelin is a substance that is wrapped around and protects the nerves—like plastic insulation protecting telephone lines. Once the myelin and the myelin-making cells are destroyed by disease in humans, they cannot be replaced. Researchers at the University of Wisconsin-Madison have managed to transplant myelin-making cells in laboratory animals. If such technology

Although most people with MS manage to find ways to accomplish daily tasks, scientists are searching for methods to prevent the disease altogether.

can be applied to humans with MS, doctors could find out where the damage had occurred. Doctors would then transplant myelin-making cells to repair the damage, essentially returning the patient to normal.[3]

At the Brookdale Center for Molecular Biology in New York City, Dr. Robert Lazzarini is trying to learn how the myelin-making cells, known as oligodendrocytes, operate. When a child is growing in the uterus of the mother, oligodendrocytes recognize the naked nerve endings that need protection. So these oligodendrocytes begin producing myelin to cover the nerves. They continue this job until about age three and then go into a maintenance phase, producing less and less myelin.

Lazzarini, working with a grant from the National Multiple Sclerosis Society and the National Institute of Neurologic Disorders and Stroke, said the goal of his work is to learn how to stimulate precursor cells to become oligodendrocytes. Precursor cells have not yet selected a path of development. They can either become neurons or become oligodendrocytes. If a person has MS, that person is losing myelin. Lazzarini said if the precursor cells can be stimulated to become oligodendrocytes, it might be possible for these cells to produce enough myelin to cover the naked nerves and prevent further attacks of MS.

The Role of Estrogen

The high occurrence of multiple sclerosis among women suggests that sex hormones may play a role in the disease.

Researchers are investigating the role that estrogen plays in MS. Estrogen is one of the hormones that regulates the immune system and is found in high levels in women who are pregnant. Pregnancy is typically the time when MS goes into remission. Researchers at the University of Southern California are trying to determine how different amounts of estrogen influence the immune system. Is it possible that low levels of estrogen could excite cells in such a way that MS flares occur? Or could altering the time and amount of hormone released in the body change the course of these attacks?[4]

Recent studies have reported that pregnancy seems to protect a person against MS flare-ups. However, following delivery of the child, the disease returns and continues in its natural course.[5]

Researchers are seeking to find out whether there is a substance released during pregnancy that stalls MS. If such a chemical exists, scientists would like to see whether that chemical can be reproduced as a drug and given to MS patients to prevent further attacks of the disease.[6]

Using Mice for MS Clues

In a laboratory in Chicago, researchers have found a way to breed mice to be susceptible to diseases that mimic multiple sclerosis. These "animal models" of MS provide scientists with the opportunity to study what causes the disease and may give hints about how to treat the disease.

Dr. Stephen Miller, from the Department of

The hormone estrogen may play a role in the higher incidence of multiple sclerosis in women.

Microbiology-Immunology at the Northwestern University Medical School, said he and his colleagues have now reached the point where they can actually prevent the mice from suffering MS-like relapses and can treat the mice that have established disease. By developing substances that attach to certain chemicals on cells, the relapses may be prevented.[7]

Miller said scientists now have to see whether the treatment that works in mice models can be adapted to the more complicated physiology of human beings.

Many Different Therapy Approaches

Scientists are looking at almost seventy different drugs that may be used in treating people with the various forms of multiple sclerosis. Not all these drugs will prove to be successful. Doctors say that any additions to the available drugs for treatment of MS will be welcome. It is also possible that researchers will learn how to use combinations of multiple sclerosis therapies to achieve better results. Doctors already know that combinations of drugs work better in treating cancer, high blood pressure, AIDS, and other illnesses.[8]

For the 350,000 people in the United States and hundreds of thousands of others throughout the world, the work of scientists who are probing the mysteries of multiple sclerosis is inching along at a very slow pace. But progress continues to be made every day. The answer to multiple sclerosis is out there.

When you have children of your own, researchers hope that multiple sclerosis will be as foreign to them as polio—a scourge of the 1940s and 1950s—is to you.

Q & A

Q. Can I catch MS from a friend whose mother or father has the disease?

A. No. MS is not infectious. You cannot catch it from someone who coughs on you, touches you, hugs you, or kisses you.

Q. If my mother has MS, will I get the disease?

A. There is an indication that MS can run in families. But 96 to 98 percent of children whose parents have MS never develop the disease.

Q. Is the number of people who contract MS increasing?

A. Some studies seem to show an increase in the number of cases of MS. But that may be due to the fact that more people now undergo magnetic resonance imaging (MRI) tests after a first attack. These tests can pinpoint MS earlier.

Q. I have heard that certain kinds of dental fillings are linked to MS. Is that true?

A. Studies by such organizations as the American Dental Association have found that the amount of mercury in dental fillings has no impact on the nervous system or the development or progression of MS. People with MS who have undergone the painful and expensive process of having their fillings replaced have not shown any improvement of their disease.

Q. Is there any link between MS and "Mad Cow Disease"?

A. Some researchers have looked at links between the process of MS in which myelin is destroyed in the brain and the human form of "mad cow disease" in which brain tissue is also destroyed. However, there does not seem to be any association between the two diseases.

Q. Is there any connection between multiple sclerosis and polluted streams or creeks?

A. When clusters of MS cases occur on an island or in a school or in a community, people try to find links with environmental triggers. An environmental trigger is a toxin—a bacterium, virus, or other substance—that unleashes the process that creates MS. So far there has been no success in finding those links. A more likely cause of these clusters is the fact that people in these clusters tend to have similar genetics that put them at risk for developing the disease.

Q. My mother says she has heard that drinking coffee or drinking soda containing caffeine causes MS. Should we avoid caffeine?

A. Because caffeine, especially in coffee, tea, and soft drinks, is ingested by so many people in the world, everyone who has any disease considers that caffeine may be a culprit. No scientific studies have been able to definitely say that caffeine causes any disease, although excess caffeine can cause sleeplessness or jitteriness.

Q. Does smoking help prevent MS?

A. No. Studies actually seem to indicate that smoking cigarettes makes symptoms of MS worse, especially hindering the ability to use the arms and legs.

Q. A friend of mine has MS. She says her father was exposed to chemicals in Vietnam when he was in the service there and that exposure led to MS. Is that possible?

A. There is no known link to MS from exposure to chemicals such as Agent Orange in Vietnam, nor to chemicals unleashed more recently during the Gulf War.

Q. Can I prevent MS by eating the right foods?

A. A healthy diet is good for you, but there is no indication that any kind of diet program is able to prevent the disease from occurring.

Q. Is exercise okay for people with MS?

A. People with MS are encouraged to exercise as much as they can, but they have to be careful not to exhaust themselves. People with MS should discuss new exercise programs with their doctors before attempting them.

Multiple Sclerosis Timeline

785—The Vikings of Scandinavia begin a series of raids that lasted four hundred years.

1822—Sir Augustus D'Este of Great Britain begins recording symptoms of his disease, the first documented case of multiple sclerosis.

1837—Sir Robert Carswell of London, professor of pathologic anatomy at University College, published the first anatomical description of MS.

1839—Jean Cruveilhier of Paris publishes illustrations similar to those of Carswell; Cruveilhier also publishes a clinical history of patients alongside autopsy findings.

1862—Jean-Martin Charcot begins work at Salpetriere Hospital in Paris, studying the drawings and observations of Carswell and Cruveilhier.

1868—Charcot calls the puzzling neurological disease "multiple sclerosis."

1878—Myelin, the substance that protects nerve fibers, is discovered.

1886—The first case of multiple sclerosis is reported in Australia.

1916—Scientists described microscopic details of how the basic processes of MS affect brain tissue.

1946—The National Multiple Sclerosis Society is founded.

1981—The invention of the magnetic resonance imaging (MRI) machine gives doctors a tool to see into the brain and help diagnose multiple sclerosis.

1993—Betaseron (interferon beta-1b) is approved as the first drug that could actively treat and alter the course of MS.

1996—The second and third drugs to treat MS—Avonex (interferon beta-1a) and Copaxone—are approved by the FDA. In Canada, interferon beta-1a is marketed as Rebif® by Serono Laboratories.

For More Information

Berlex Laboratories
300 Fairfield Road
Wayne, NJ 07470
Patient Support Program
"Multiple Sclerosis Pathways"
1-800-788-1467
http://www.betaseron.com

Biogen, Inc.
14 Cambridge Center
Cambridge, MA 02142
Patient Support Program
"Avonex Support Line"
1-800-456-2255
http://www.biogen.com

International Multiple Sclerosis Support Foundation
P.O. Box 90154
Tucson, AZ 85752-0154

The Multiple Sclerosis Association of America
706 Haddonfield Road
Cherry Hill, NJ 08002
1-800-LEARN-MS

National Multiple Sclerosis Society
733 Third Avenue
New York, NY 10017-3288
1-800-FIGHT-MS
http://www.nmss.org

National Rehabilitation Information Center
8455 Colesville Road, Suite 935
Silver Spring, MD 20910-3319

Teva Marion Partners
P.O. Box 9813
10236 Marion Park Drive
Kansas City, MO 64134-0627
Patient Support Program
1-800-887-8100
http://www.tevamarionpartners.com

Chapter Notes

Chapter 1. What Is Happening to Me?

1. Roger Kennedy's story is one of several stories of persons who have multiple sclerosis. The stories were distributed as part of the May 1996 press kit promoting the availability of Avonex, manufactured by Biogen Inc., Cambridge, Massachusetts.

2. Arney Rosenblat, "Multiple Sclerosis," Multiple sclerosis media fact sheet, National Multiple Sclerosis Society, February 1997.

Chapter 2. MS: A New Disease or an Old One?

1. Personal interview with Dr. Stephen Reingold of the National Multiple Sclerosis Society in New York, June 25, 1998.

2. "Multiple Sclerosis: A History of the Disease," *MS Society of Victoria*, March 6, 1997, <http://home.vicnet.net.au/~mssvic/erisch1.html> (September 16, 1998).

3. Robert Berkow, ed., *The Merck Manual of Diagnosis and Therapy*, 16th ed. (Rahway, N.J.: Merck Research Laboratories, 1992), p. 2393.

4. C.M. Poser, "The Dissemination of Multiple Sclerosis: A Viking Saga? A Historical Essay," *Annals of Neurology*, December 1994, 36 Supplement 2, pp. 231–243.

5. Interview with Reingold.

6. *MS Society of Victoria.*

7. "Multiple Sclerosis," *Baylor College of Medicine, Department of Neurology*, n.d., <http://www.bcm.tmc.edu/neurol/struct/ms/ms2.html> (September 16, 1998).

8. Christine Loveland, "Race, Culture, and Disability," American Psychological Association annual meeting presentation, August 10–14, 1996, Toronto.

9. Loren Rolak, *Research Highlights*, newsletter of the NMSS Research and Medical Programs, Winter/Spring 1996, p. 3.

10. Dylan Humphrey, "My Own Road Through MS . . . ," July 21, 1998, <http://www.sccs.swarthmore.edu~dylan/ms/> (September 16, 1998).

Chapter 3. What Is Multiple Sclerosis?

1. Suzanne M. Jackson, "Ex-legislator Goike Remains Active Despite MS," *Syracuse Herald-Journal*, December 19, 1997, p. C10.

2. "Research Changing How Doctors View Multiple Sclerosis," *Doctor's Guide to Medical and Other News,* n.d., <http://www.pslgroup.com/dg/53a46/htm> (September 16, 1998).

3. Bruce Trapp, "Axonal Transection in the Lesions of Multiple Sclerosis," *New England Journal of Medicine*, January 29, 1998, pp. 278–285.

4. Fred Lubin and Stephen Reingold, "Defining the Clinical Course of Multiple Sclerosis: Results of an International Study," *Neurology*, April 1996, pp. 907–911, excerpted in "Promise and Progress in MS Treatment," *National MS Society*, 1997 Teleconference program book, pp. 11–15.

5. Betty A. Iams, "Betty's House . . . Life After MS," August 22, 1998, <http://home.san.rr.com/iamshouse/> (September 16, 1998).

6. Personal interview with Dr. Stephen Reingold of the National Multiple Sclerosis Society in New York, June 25, 1998.

7. Pam Iannello's story is one of several stories of persons who have multiple sclerosis. The stories were distributed as part of the May 1996 press kit promoting the availability of Avonex, manufactured by Biogen Inc., Cambridge, Massachusetts.

8. Robert Cooke, "Study: Herpes Virus May Cause MS," *The Palm Beach Post*, November 27, 1997, p. 30A.

9. Interview with Reingold.

10. J.H.D. Millar, *Multiple Sclerosis: A Disease Acquired in Childhood* (Springfield, Ill.: Charles C. Thomas Publishers, 1971), pp. 60–62.

11. Randy Schapiro, "What Virus Causes MS?," n.d., <http://www.htinet.com/msen/causes5.html> (September 16, 1998).

12. Ibid.

Chapter 4. Symptoms of Multiple Sclerosis

1. "Information About MS," *MS Society of Canada-Saskatchewan Division Page*, n.d., <http://www.usak.ca/anatomy/msinfo.html> (February 14, 1998).

2. J.H.D. Millar, *Multiple Sclerosis: A Disease Acquired in Childhood* (Springfield, Ill.: Charles C. Thomas Publishers, 1971), pp. 60–62.

3. John Pekkanen, "A Champion's Vow," *Reader's Digest,* February 1998, pp. 76–83.

4. Susan Wells, *Multiple Sclerosis: Managing Symptoms* (Cherry Hill, N.J.: Multiple Sclerosis Association of America, 1996), pp. 5–6.

5. Kathryn Knight, "Crown Tells Jury to Clear Killer Driver," *The Times* (London), March 20, 1998, Home News Section.

6. Wells, pp. 5–6.

7. Ibid.

8. Pekkanen, p. 79.

9. Tara Sullivan, "Hooping for Her Health," *Daily News* (New York), December 8, 1996, p. 95.

10. Telephone interview with Shirlene Warnock, March 23, 1998.

11. Michele Overgard, "Recovering from an Attack: The Uninvited Guest," *Inside MS*, Fall 1997/Winter 1998, pp. 8–13.

12. Ibid.

Chapter 5. Diagnosis of Multiple Sclerosis

1. Douglas McAlpine, Charles Lumsden, and E. D. Acheson, *Multiple Sclerosis: A Reappraisal* (Baltimore, Md.: The Williams and Wilkins Company, 1972), p. 132.

2. Loren Rolak, "MS History Fact," *Research Highlights*, newsletter of the NMSS Research and Medical Programs, Winter/Spring 1996, p. 8.

3. Roy L. Swank, *A Biochemical Basis of Multiple Sclerosis* (Springfield, Ill.: Charles C. Thomas Publishers, 1961), p. 6.

4. Personal interview with Dr. Stephen Reingold of the National Multiple Sclerosis Society in New York, June 25, 1998.

5. "Is Multiple Sclerosis a Possibility?" Cherry Hill, N.J.: Multiple Sclerosis Association of America, undated.

6. J.H.D. Millar, *Multiple Sclerosis: A Disease Acquired in Childhood* (Springfield, Ill.: Charles C. Thomas, 1971), pp. 53–55.

Chapter 6. Treatment of Multiple Sclerosis

1. Interviews during 1998 with friends of "Nancy" who wish to remain anonymous.

2. Susan Wells, *Multiple Sclerosis: Managing Symptoms* (Cherry Hill, N.J.: Multiple Sclerosis Association of America, 1996), pp. 5–7.

3. Ibid.

4. Douglas McAlpine, Charles Lumsden, and E. D. Acheson, *Multiple Sclerosis: A Reappraisal* (Baltimore, Md.: The Williams and Wilkins Company, 1972), pp. 168–170.

5. Wells, pp. 9–15.

6. Jane Halper and Nancy Holland, *Comprehensive Nursing Care in Multiple Sclerosis* (New York: Demos Vermande, 1996), pp. 27–30.

7. Wells, pp. 15–27.

8. Randall Schapiro, "Is MS Inherited?" *The Betaseron MS Resource Center*, October 1995, <http://www.betaseron.com/messages/messages3/m3qanda.html> (April 17, 1998).

9. Wells, pp. 15–27.

10. Stephen Reingold, "Additional Safety and Efficacy Data Reported for Betaseron," *Promise and Progress in MS Treatment* (New York: National MS Society, 1997), Teleconference program book, pp. 16–18.

11. Stephen Reingold, "Update on Neutralizing Antibodies Against Interferon Beta-1b (Betaseron)," *Promise and Progress in MS Treatment* (New York: National MS Society, 1997), Teleconference program book, pp. 19–20.

12. Abe Eastwood and Stephen Reingold, "FDA Approves Biogen's Avonex (interferon beta-1a) for Relapsing Forms of MS," *Promise and Progress in MS Treatment* (New York: National MS Society, 1997), Teleconference program book, pp. 21–22.

13. Ed Susman, "Net Surfers Wiping Out Under Waves of Hyped Biotech Drug Info," *Biotechnology Newswatch*, September 2, 1996.

14. "New Study Provides More Evidence that Copaxone Can Slow Progression of Multiple Sclerosis and Reduces Attacks," University of Maryland Medical Center press release, March 23, 1998.

15. Ed Susman, "FDA Approves New Drug for MS," *United Press International*, December 23, 1996.

16. Personal interview with Dr. Kenneth Johnson during the American Academy of Neurology annual meeting, Minneapolis, Minn., May 2, 1998.

17. University of Maryland Medical Center press release.

Chapter 7. MS Can Hurt Those Who Do Not Have It

1. "MS Through the Eyes of a Child," National Multiple Sclerosis Society, 1997. The "MS Through the Eyes of a Child" program included comments, drawings, and pictures of children whose parents or loved ones have MS. The work of the children was used to produce a calendar, greeting cards, and note cards.

2. Ibid.

3. Ibid.

4. Telephone interview with Shirlene Warnock, March 23, 1998.

5. Pamela Cavallo, *When a Parent Has MS: A Teenager's Guide*, National MS Society, 1995, pp. 18–19.

6. Mike Tolson, "Praise and Prayer: Friends Say Farewell to Barbara Jordan," *Houston Chronicle home page*, <http://www.chron.com/content/chronicle/page1/96/01/21/mainbar2.html> (January 20,1996).

7. "Richard Pryor: Comic on the Edge," A&E Television Network's *Biography* Web page, <http://www.biography.com/cgi-bin/biomain.cgi> (December 23, 1998).

8. "Annette Funicello," *Biography.watch*, August 16, 1996, <http://www.biography.com/watch/listings/annette.html> (April 17, 1998).

9. "Walker Diagnosed with MS," *Associated Press*, April 27, 1996.

10. Lois Romano, "The Prosecutor at Ground Zero," *The Washington Post*, March 31, 1997, p. D1.

11. Kim Michaud Wheelock, "Alan R. Osmond," Osmond Communications LLC media release, 1997.

12. "MS Though the Eyes of a Child."

Chapter 8. A Future Without Multiple Sclerosis?

1. Stephen Reingold and Arney Rosenblat, "MS Research into the Year 2000 and Beyond," National Multiple Sclerosis Society press release, 1997.

2. "Suspicion Mounts on Herpes Virus in MS," *Research Highlights*, National MS Society, Summer/Fall 1997, pp. 4–6.

3. Personal interview with Dr. Robert Lazzarini, August 11, 1998.

4. Stephen Reingold and Cathy Carlson, "Summary of Research Progress—1997," *Research Programs Department News*, National Multiple Sclerosis Society.

5. Gene Emery, "Risk of MS Relapse Wanes During Pregnancy," *Reuters*, July 29, 1998.

6. Personal interview with Arney Rosenblat of the National Multiple Sclerosis Society, August 12, 1998.

7. Personal interview with Dr. Stephen Miller, August 12, 1998.

8. Reingold and Rosenblat, press release.

Glossary

acute—Having a short but intense or severe duration.

AIDS—Acquired immunodeficiency syndrome. A condition in which HIV causes the body's immune system to fail, allowing a person to become infected with various diseases.

amyotrophic lateral sclerosis—A disease in which nerves that control the lungs and heart are destroyed, eventually leading to death; it is also named Lou Gehrig's disease after the famous baseball player who died from it.

anemia—A lower than normal level of cells in the blood that carry oxygen, which can make people feel weak and look pale.

antibodies—Proteins in the blood that act as an immune defense.

autoimmune disease—A disease state in which chemicals in the body attack healthy tissue instead of attacking bad invaders.

autopsy—The inspection and dissection of a body after death in order to determine causes of death.

Avonex—One of the drugs used to control and prevent new attacks of multiple sclerosis. Its main ingredient is called interferon beta-1a.

bacteria—Any microscopic one-celled organisms that may be involved in infectious diseases.

Betaseron—A drug used to prevent recurrent attacks of multiple sclerosis. Its main ingredient is called interferon beta-1b.

biotechnology—The use of living organisms in the production of medications.

bladder—The organ that collects and holds urine.

botulin—A deadly poison, which in very small amounts can be used to control muscle spasms in people with multiple sclerosis.

cancer—A growth in the body that can invade other organs.

caregivers—People such as doctors, nurses, friends, and family members who take care of others who have diseases.

chronic—Having a long duration.

Copaxone—A drug used to reduce or prevent further MS attacks. Its main ingredient is called glatiramer acetate.

diabetes—A disease in which the body no longer produces enough insulin to use up sugars in the blood.

dormant—Lacking activity or growth.

estrogen—A hormone that is found in all women.

exacerbations—The acute attacks of multiple sclerosis.

gene—A group of molecules that instruct the formation of proteins that, in turn, provide the elements that make the body function in distinct ways.

genome—The entire genetic information contained in a cell.

herpes—A virus responsible for several diseases, including mouth blisters, chicken pox, and roseola.

HIV—Human immunodeficiency virus, the virus that causes AIDS. HIV is infectious and contagious, but only through specific kinds of contact.

hormone—Compounds produced in organs that regulate levels of fluids in the body.

immune system—The complex function of the body that allows cells to react to disease.

inflammation—Redness or swelling in a certain area of the body, often occurring with pain, fever, and the reduced ability to use parts of the body.

insulin—A hormone that regulates levels of sugar and other chemicals in the body.

interferons—A group of substances in the body that can improve the immune system function; both Betaseron® and Avonex® are interferon-based medications.

intramuscular injection—A procedure in which medication is given by a needle into a muscle.

leukemia—A type of cancer in which blood cells are overproduced.

Lyme disease—An infectious disease spread by a bacterium found in deer ticks.

magnetic resonance imaging (MRI)—A procedure used in medicine for producing images of tissues inside the body without opening the body through surgery.

multiple sclerosis—A disease of the central nervous system characterized by attacks that can affect every organ of the body.

myelin—A soft, white, fatty material in the membrane of certain cells in the nervous system that makes up the covering of nerves.

neurological diseases—Illnesses involving the nerves, such as multiple sclerosis.

neurologist—A doctor who specializes in treating people with nervous system disorders.

neutralizing proteins—Antibodies that develop with use of certain drugs used in treating multiple sclerosis.

optic nerve—The nerve that connects the eye to the brain and makes vision possible.

optic neuritis—Inflammation of the optic nerve.

paralysis—The inability to move.

Parkinson's disease—A condition in which a person suffers from uncontrollable tremors and rigidity of the arms, legs, and head.

placebo—A false medication used as a control when testing a new drug's effectiveness.

placebo effect—A phenomenon in which people feel better when given false medication.

polio—A crippling, sometimes fatal disease that often occurred in children in the 1940s and 1950s but has virtually been eliminated through vaccination programs today.

quadriceps—A major muscle in the upper thigh.

relapse—Recurrence of a disease after a period of remission.

remission—A period during which a disease temporarily subsides or decreases in its effects on people.

retrobulbar neuritis—A condition that occurs when a part of the optic nerve becomes inflamed.

rheumatoid arthritis—A chronic disease in which the joints of the body become inflamed and deformed.

roseola—A rash that occurs in response to viral infection.

spasm—An involuntary movement of a muscle.

spasticity—A condition that occurs in people with multiple sclerosis in which their hands or legs may suddenly jerk out of control.

steroids—A class of medications that is used to treat various symptoms of multiple sclerosis, including vision problems caused by inflammation.

subcutaneous injection—A procedure in which medication is delivered through a needle inserted just under the skin.

symptom—A condition that arises from a certain disease.

tremor—The involuntary shaking of parts of the body.

virus—A very small organism that invades living cells and reproduces itself.

Further Reading

Books

Carroll, David L., and Jon Dudley Dorman. *Living Well with Multiple Sclerosis: A Guide for Patient, Caregiver, & Family*. New York: HarperPerennial, 1993.

Gold, Susan D. *Multiple Sclerosis*. Parsippany, N.J.: Silver Burdett Press, 1996.

Kalb, Rosalind C., ed. *Multiple Sclerosis: The Questions You Have, The Answers You Need*. New York: Demos Vermandes, 1996.

Lechtenberg, Richard. *Multiple Sclerosis Fact Book*. 2nd ed. Philadelphia: F.A. Davis Company, 1995.

Rosner, Louis J., and Shelley Ross. *Multiple Sclerosis*. New York: Simon & Schuster, 1992.

Scheinberg, Labe C. *Multiple Sclerosis: A Guide for Patients and Their Families*. 2nd ed. Philadelphia: Lippincott-Raven Publishers, 1996.

Shuman, Robert, and Janice Schwartz. *Living with Multiple Sclerosis: A Handbook for Families*. New York: Macmillan Publishing Company, Inc., 1994.

Internet Addresses

The Internet is a marvelous resource for finding information about multiple sclerosis, but remember that information on the Internet is not screened or edited. The information can come from doctors, patients, nurses, or anyone else who wants to discuss MS. All information found on the Internet should be discussed with a competent, knowledgeable medical professional before incorporating that information in a treatment program.

Berlex Laboratories, Inc. *The Betaseron MS Resource Center.* 1997. <http://www.betaseron.com> (February 24, 1999).

CLAMS. *Computer Literate Advocates for Multiple Sclerosis.* June 4, 1996. <http://www.clams.org> (February 24, 1999).

Halko, Aapo. "MS Info Links." *MS Crossroads.* n.d. <www.helsinki.fi/~ahalko/ms.html> (February 24, 1999).

IMSSF. *International Multiple Sclerosis Support Foundation.* 1996–1999. <http://aspin.asu.edu/msnews/indexa.htm> (February 24, 1999).

The Myelin Project. n.d. <http://www.myelin.org> (February 24, 1999).

SoftWatch Ltd. *MS Watch*™. 1998. <http://www.mswatch.com/> (February 24, 1999).

Index

ML   6/01